DAY BOMBER

Arthur Eyton-Jones

SUTTON PUBLISHING

First published in the United Kingdom in 1998 by
Sutton Publishing Limited · Phoenix Mill
Thrupp · Stroud · Gloucestershire · GL5 2BU

British Library Cataloguing in Publication Data
A catalogue record for this book is available from the British Library.

ISBN 0-7509-1850-0

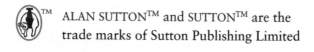 ALAN SUTTON™ and SUTTON™ are the
trade marks of Sutton Publishing Limited

Typeset in 10/13pt Sabon.
Typesetting and origination by
Sutton Publishing Limited.
Printed in Great Britain by
MPG Books, Bodmin, Cornwall.

Contents

Prologue

Briefing completed, parachute harness on, flying helmet, navigator's green bag filled with maps, etc., and last but not least parachute clutched in either hand – and out to the crew bus which drops us off at our aircraft's dispersal point. We are flying an American Boston, unusual for its tricycle undercarriage and the fact that all three crew members are in separate compartments and cannot reach each other. My entry is a small hatch under the nose and just in front of the nosewheel. It is slammed shut by an obliging member of the groundcrew and I am alone in the nose with a bulletproof bulkhead behind me and a Mk IV bomb-sight in front. Pull down the hinged plywood map table across my lap and I am sitting very much like a baby in its high chair! After having secured my parachute in its storage space and laid out maps, pencils, instruments, etc., I plug into the intercommunication socket and contact the rest of the crew.

At engine start-up time the twin 1,600 h.p. Wright-Cyclone radial engines burst into life with a shattering roar and in due course we leave our dispersal and take our place in the queue of aircraft taxiing round the perimeter track. The leader takes us over the centre of base and down we go to low level and head for the coast. Being a new crew we are 'tailend charlie', that is to say at the rear of the formation. Our meeting point with our Spitfire escort is at Beachy Head, and what a sight meets my eyes: squadron after squadron of Spitfires circling and wheeling around at a very low level. We flash over Beachy Head and dive down to sea level, our escort of Spitfires falling in close on either side, their pilots grinning at us and giving thumbs-up signs, a lovely sight. There is another high-level escort way above us but we cannot see them.

The sea flashes past under the nose. Ten minutes from the enemy coast throttles are pushed forward and up we climb at 1,000 feet per minute, the surface of the sea dropping away beneath us, so that we can cross the coast at 10,000 feet. Up at this height I feel not a little conspicuous and as we cross the coast look down and see the flashes coming from the anti-aircraft guns as they fire at us. All too soon the black flak bursts all around us and the leader takes the formation in avoiding action, up and down and side to side, but only gently because of our Spitfire escort. They told me that if you can hear the crack of the explosion over the noise of the engines it is close; if you can see the red in the centre of the explosion it is very close; and if you can smell the cordite, it is too close. They were right!

As the target approaches I fold back my map table, lean forward and adjust the bomb-sight for height, course, speed, wind, etc., and wait for the leading navigator to come on the radio, which he does with the words 'Bomb doors open'. In a Boston the pilot opens the bomb doors and from the rear of the formation I can see that they have done so. The Spitfires pull away to one side, very sensibly, as this is where the flak will really be intense as we weave into the attack. For at least fifteen seconds we have to fly perfectly straight and level and I can see the target sliding into view down the drift-wires of my bomb-sight. 'Bombs gone' from the leading navigator, and I press the button held in my right hand. Looking down, our bombs seem almost stationary in relation to ourselves, then when they have fallen further they seem to shoot ahead as they are seen in relation to the ground. Finally, as their noses drop, they disappear from sight until the bursts can be seen on the ground. 'Bomb doors closed' and a diving turn away from the target, our Spitfires rejoining us. Back to the coast, more flak and noses down for the sea, but not too fast otherwise we would lose our escort who have to continually weave, watching for enemy fighters behind them.

Skim over the waves, then the wonderful sight of the white cliffs of Dover ahead. Our escort peel away to return to their own bases and we head for home at a more reasonable height of 1,000 feet. Another operation completed.

They were not always so easy.

Preface

This is not a story of the grand strategy of the Second World War nor is it one in which the writer can show how he mixed with the famous personages of those times. In fact it is only the simple and very personal story of how the war affected me. I must admit to thoroughly enjoying writing it and have only done so because 'The War' is no longer a fashionable subject for conversation.

During all the time I served in the Royal Air Force I and my comrades were aware, through the media of the radio and the newspapers, that great and world-shaking events were taking place and that the war news was, for the most part, bad; but I can honestly say that I do not think for a minute any of us doubted that we would win in the end and I also think that to each of us our personal, limited view of the war was far more important to us than the major events that happened around us. As an example, the fall of Singapore came at the time I had finished my training in South Africa and was about to return to England. This fact was far more important to me than all the disasters in the Far East.

Finally, on reflection, the writing of this book has made me realise how I changed over those years from a very keen young airman to a rather sad (the friends that were killed always seemed to be the best) and worn-out flight lieutenant.

CHAPTER 1

AC2 Wireless Operator – 1940

As I write, a very battered RAF Form 2168 lies on the table beside me; it is headed 'Royal Air Force Volunteer Reserve' and the thing that I was intensely proud of at the time was the big rubber-stamped 'VOLUNTEER' over the heading. The date on the form is 9 October 1939. On being asked what branch of the Service I wished to join I immediately replied 'Aircrew', but was told that there was a waiting list of up to six months for pilots and navigators. At the age of nineteen six months is an eternity and my spirits sank – but wait, the ever-helpful recruiting sergeant had a solution: if I enrolled as a wireless operator there would be every opportunity on the course to remuster (strange words then) to aircrew, so wireless operator it was. It only remained to break the news gently to my parents and the constabulary by whom I was then employed; both took it very well.

It was the first week of January 1940 before the long-awaited instructions arrived – report to RAF Station, Padgate, near Warrington.

The atmosphere of the time seemed to infect all recruits alike and we were indeed a mixed bunch. The RAF took us under its capable wing from the minute we arrived. None of the oft-heard jokes regarding badly fitting kit seemed to apply to us and I remember that our only worry in that direction was the possibility of receiving the old 'dog collar' type of tunic which was still being issued at that time; otherwise as in all other things our kit was issued with speed and efficiency. One had the feeling that the Service had done all this before many times, the only difference at present being that it was obviously overwhelmed by the number of bodies with which it had to cope. This was borne out by the fact that the first few nights were spent sleeping on the floor of the gym on issue 'biscuits', that is three individual squares which when placed together formed a mattress.

Those of us who had volunteered proudly stitched the letters 'VR' on our shoulders using the housewife provided by a thoughtful country. New songs were learned and sung with gusto, one of the favourites being 'The Quartermaster's Stores'. After Padgate I was posted to No. 2 Wireless School, Yatesbury.

Royal Air Force Station, Yatesbury, is, or was, situated on the side of a ridge of the Wiltshire Downs just above the small market town of Calne, on the main A4 road to Marlborough, Newbury and Reading.

As the course progressed we became more and more 'Morse happy' until the great day arrived when after a cursory medical examination we split up into ground and aircrew operators. Much to my joy I joined the aircrew operators and all-too-brief visits were made to rooms in which aircraft sets had been mounted with dummy aerials for limited distance transmitting and receiving. By modern standards these sets were old-fashioned indeed, being the TR9 air-to-ground radio telephone transmitter/receiver with a range of about five miles if you were lucky, and the 'Jeep' set 1082/1083 for air-to-ground Morse transmission and reception with a range of about one hundred miles. Nevertheless we regarded them with awe, and spirits were so high that one night we even had a pillow fight.

The historic events which were occurring over the Channel meant nothing to us; the next Morse test was a subject of far more interest. Only when we were advised not to visit the south coast as it was rumoured that Army Dunkirk veterans were in the habit of beating up RAF men did we pause to consider that this was hardly fair, in our case anyway.

Came the great day when we were due for our first flight. We were taken to the nearby flying field on a lorry and split into teams of six. In single file, like a bunch of convicts, we were marched into the parachute section and each fitted with a combined parachute harness and one-piece flying suit which was the most revolting thing I ever came across. It was made of a rubbery material and was exceedingly hot to wear in that lovely summer weather; luckily I never saw these suits again.

It was at this point in our training that some of us were called together and asked whether we would like to volunteer for special duties. No mention was made as to what these duties were to be and it shows how much we were all still under the spell of that word that without exception we all said yes. Nothing more was heard of this incident and indeed I had forgotten all about it until the day our course, having passed out, received posting notices to Air Gunnery School. This would be a four-week course and then we would all be able to sew on the coveted air gunner's brevet and a set of sergeant's stripes to match. Imagine my surprise when I found that once again I was on my own and no posting had come through for me. On enquiry at the orderly room I was told by that fount of all wisdom, the orderly room clerk, that I had been selected for a navigation course. At that time there was an urgent need for radar operators on night fighters, so I was in the position of 'Awaiting Posting'.

Eventually the wheels of Air Ministry Records ground into action and the orderly room clerk informed me that I was posted to No. 1 S of GR at Squires Gate, Blackpool. On enquiry nobody knew what the initials S of GR stood for and the nearest anyone could suggest was School of Ground Radio, so it was with a heavy heart that I made my way to Squires Gate on 11 September 1940.

Squires Gate was – I don't know what it is now as I have never visited it since – a small grass aerodrome on the southern outskirts of Blackpool. Here I found that No. 1 S of GR stood for No. 1 School of General Reconnaissance and was a training unit in navigation for navigators of Coastal Command. It consisted of a wholly regular unit flying old Ansons fitted with gun turrets and no flaps. On reporting to the orderly room I was asked whether I wished to be a ground wireless operator or to fly; the answer was obvious but the question itself gave me a nasty jolt as it showed that I was regarded as just another wireless operator.

With some misgivings I made my way to A Flight Hangar Wireless Section to report to a Corporal Newby DFM i/c Wireless Section A Flight. Corporal Newby was a stocky man with a fierce expression, rather protruding blue eyes and wearing on his tunic a dirty piece of ribbon from which I could not take my eyes, the DFM. He took me under his capable wing and saw that I was issued with a flying helmet, black leather flying boots, a one-piece flying suit of far better pattern than the Yatesbury variety, a pair of leather gauntlets and a flying logbook (which I have to this day). As a wireless operator I was instructed in the method of assembling the earphones and microphone and shown how to tape the plug which connected it all to the aircraft system so that it would not get broken, as often happened to the more ignorant other aircrew trades. My cup of happiness was full to overflowing. For the next week I was fully employed – sweeping the hangar floor.

On 18 September 1940, at 1015 hours according to my logbook, I flew for the first time as a real wireless operator in Anson K8815, Pilot Officer Sutton-Jones at the controls.

Rumour soon turned to fact and we were all issued with tropical kit complete with topee: the unit was going overseas. This called for another visit to the orderly room where I was informed in tones of great sarcasm that 'Yes, they knew that I was awaiting a navigation course'; they then went on to elaborate: 'Had I not heard of the newly started Empire Air Training Scheme? I had? Then how did I think I was going to get there, on a boat of my own? Air Ministry had obviously attached me to this unit knowing its destination and my posting would be arranged the other end.' (I was to go out on the first echelon.) All this sounded most logical to my innocent mind and I went on embarkation leave much cheered.

On returning to Squires Gate after our leave we were handed over to the tender care of the medical branch who proceeded with reckless abandon to stick needles into both arms of all concerned. A special troop train was scheduled to take us on the first stage of the journey to our unknown destination at midnight.

In the early hours of the morning our train halted at a station which turned out to be Greenock, near Glasgow, and a tired and hungry bunch of airmen tumbled out on to a cold and dark platform. With a feeling of deep gratitude we collected round the trolleys supervised by that fine body of women the WVS and had a hot cup of tea and a bun each, all free. This turned out to be our breakfast and shortly afterwards we were herded on to a ferry and taken out to that beautiful liner the *Cape Town Castle* which was moored out in the Clyde. This was the *Cape Town Castle*'s first venture into the trooping business and she was in fine condition. We sailed the next morning in a fast convoy consisting of the *Cape Town Castle, The Georgic,* and the *Windsor Castle;* our escort comprised one city class cruiser and six destroyers. I have always loved the sea and am lucky in being a good sailor. We made an uneventful trip to Cape Town.

The wonders of Cape Town and the Table Mountain are well known but we did not have time to appreciate them as we were put straight into a special train awaiting us at the docks and off we went inland. Eventually the train jerked to a halt at the little town of George, which is by the sea in Cape Province. What a welcome met us! All the Europeans from the town were there to greet us, complete with little Union Jacks. We were received as conquering heroes and whisked away to the town hall in a fleet of private cars to a civic reception. To a unit with our history the irony was not lost. We had just travelled seven thousand miles away from the war and here we were greeted with a heroes' reception. Afterwards we were taken in private cars some five miles out of the town to our eventual destination, to find that the only thing that had been erected on the airfield was our sleeping huts; even the cookhouse did not have a roof. The date was 29 October 1940.

CHAPTER 2

Empire Air Training Scheme, South Africa

What words can describe that beautiful, unhappy country, South Africa? Our first reaction was to revel in the sunshine, warmth, new foods, strange smells and the sound of the crickets at night. It was summer in South Africa and after wartime Britain it was truly paradise – and there was no blackout. The building of the camp proceeded rapidly; soon we had decent quarters.

The townsfolk were kindness itself and soon every airman had been 'adopted' by one family or another. I had a great friend at the time, a fellow wireless operator, and we were soon both on good terms with the proprietor of the local delicatessen. He was a short wiry Australian who had settled in South Africa after the Boer War and married a South African woman. He had only two hates, Hitler and Bing Crosby, and he and his family were kindness itself. They delighted in cooking the tastiest South African dishes for us and taking us out for picnics to see the lovely countryside.

The way these friendships were made were as follows: a car would pull up at the guardroom and the occupants would enquire whether any airmen would like to go out on a picnic. One day I happened to be the only airman at the guardroom when a native chauffeur drew up in a large car and solemnly presented a visiting card from Brigadier General Sir Ingram-Brooke. I accepted gladly, not realising at the time that this chance meeting would change the whole course of my Service life. After a very pleasant swim at the nearby beach I was taken to a charming bungalow on the outskirts of town to be greeted with real old-world courtesy by the brigadier general, his sister and a large well-mannered dog. This was the first of many very enjoyable visits.

The inside of the bungalow was furnished in typical English country house style with comfortable chintz-covered chairs, a lovely writing desk in a bay window with leaded lights and a bookcase beside the fireplace. The gardens were as neat as a new pin. The general's sister was tall and thin and always wore large wide-brimmed hats of the old style. She ruled the general, who was in poor health, with a firm but kindly hand, and I spent many pleasant evenings listening to the old man recounting his past experiences, such as the siege of Ladysmith. On the stroke of 9 p.m. his sister would quietly but firmly bring the conversation to a close and lead the old man off to bed. The manner in which these two charming people could put a shy awkward young airman second class at his ease and treat him as an honoured guest is something I will always treasure.

Eventually a party was despatched to Cape Town to assemble and fly back to us the Ansons that were arriving by sea, and it was with great excitement that we all gathered one day to greet the first planes in. Imagine the feelings of the wireless operators when we discovered that there was no wireless equipment aboard! This state of affairs lasted for some time, and the morale of the Wireless Section reached an all-time low as we were employed on sundry odd jobs. It was April 1941 before the wireless equipment arrived and we eagerly set to fitting it in the Ansons. On 16 April I took off in Anson R3395 'G' for George which subsequently became my aircraft, Pilot Officer Smith at the controls, and flew for the first time out over the Indian Ocean.

There were two things about this and subsequent trips that are perhaps worth mentioning. The first was that unlike flying in Great Britain there was no radio silence, so we had the opportunity to transmit and receive messages to base and each other continuously – and as the competition to be the fastest operator was keen we became very proficient. The second point was that whereas the pilot and pupil navigators walked away from the aircraft in lordly fashion after landing, we mere aircraftsmen had to help both refuel and push the Ansons back into the hangars before we left. Refuelling was a hot and laborious business in those early days, as it was done with the aid of a handpump fitted into a 40-gallon drum. Despite this they were happy times with a lot of good-natured chaff going on between the ground crews.

The weeks passed pleasantly enough with plenty of flying out over the ocean some hundred miles from the coast. May turned to June and June to July. The second echelon had arrived from England and brought the shattering news that two weeks after we had left they had been looking for me as my posting to a navigation course in Scotland had come through! This called for a hurried visit to the orderly room where I was shown an Air Ministry order stating that, owing to an acute shortage, wireless operators could no longer remuster! At about this time we were slowly realising that being attached to the South African Air Force had its snags. All their restrictive regulations, plus those of the RAF, applied to us it seemed, but not the advantages of either. We were no longer No. 1 School of General Reconnaissance but had been renamed No. 61 Air School.

Time passed and by August I had sat both my aircraftsman first class and leading aircraftsman trade test examinations and was a fully fledged leading aircraftsman wireless operator with a propeller sewn on each sleeve. These had been peacetime exams and although it was pointed out to me by the regulars that I was now an expert in my trade I still did not feel that I was very far up the ladder. I had served for one year and eight months, which is a long time at the age of twenty-one. I had 97 hours 40 minutes' flying time in my log and was seven thousand miles away from the war I had joined up to fight. I loved the old Anson; it was roomy, reliable and had excellent all-round visibility, but try as I might it was impossible to make her look very warlike. One evening, after yet another unsuccessful attempt to remuster to aircrew, I was feeling pretty down and must have shown it. I was visiting the old brigadier general, and his observant and kindly sister asked me why I was looking so glum. Out came my tale of woe, and much to my surprise the old man listened patiently. At the end he told me to put it all down on paper as the Under Secretary of State for Air was a friend of his. Back at camp I did as I was bid, more out of courtesy than from any hope of action, and duly handed in the sad tale on my next visit. My surprise in exactly four weeks' time knew no bounds when an awed orderly room clerk came round to my hut to inform me that a direct posting from the Air Ministry had just come through for me to proceed to a navigation course!

On 15 September I took off for the last time in good old 'G' for George with Sergeant Alt as pilot. A fortnight after I left No. 61 Air School, 'G' for George ditched in the Indian Ocean, but being a lady to the end floated for half an hour which enabled all the crew to be saved. Once again I said goodbye to all my friends and set off on my own, arriving at No. 75 Air School, Lyttelton, near Johannesburg, on 21 September. This was a barren sandy transit camp and I found myself in the company of a lot of newly arrived aircrew cadets, complete with their leading aircraftsman badges, white aircrew flashes in their caps and not more than six months' service in! They treated me with kindly condescension and started to 'gen' me up on the country, whereupon I exploded and shot a terrible line about long service etc., the outcome of which I was to regret for the rest of my stay in South Africa. I was wearing a tunic and tie at the time and I mentioned casually that this was because my blood was thin through long service in hot climates. To perpetuate this myth I endured many uncomfortable hot days in the months to come.

It was with no feeling of sorrow therefore that I received the news that I was to join a course of newly arrived cadets who had been posted to No. 45 Air School, Oudtshoorn, and at long last I placed a white aircrew flash in my cap. We arrived at Oudtshoorn on 18 October. It was a hot dusty little town situated some thirty miles inland from George over the other side of a three thousand-foot range of mountains and nothing like as pretty as George. I never made any friends there but spent every available opportunity hitch-hiking back over the mountains to George.

I can see from my logbook that we did not waste much time once we arrived at 45 Air School, as on 21 October I flew in Anson No. 1178 with Pilot Warrant Officer Truby on Exercise No. 1 Air Experience!

Flying on a navigation course was not the pleasure it had been as a wireless operator. To begin with you had a large green canvas bag filled with all the tools of your trade which you had to carry out to the aircraft; secondly, the unfortunate pupil who sat next to the pilot had to wind up the undercarriage, which in that hot climate – it was summer again – reduced the fittest to grease spots; thirdly, unlike flying from George we were over land all the time which was exceedingly bumpy, so that many of the pupils were very ill.

Towards Christmas we were coming to the end of the course and on 16 December flew on a navigation exercise to East London on the coast, taking off at 0513 hours, landing at East London and returning in the afternoon. For Christmas I went over to George but the station did not seem the same. Some of my friends had been posted and the officers were devoting all their time to their families, leaving the airmen on their own. No meals were being served in the cookhouse, you just wandered in and helped yourself to what was there while the whole camp got quietly or noisily drunk.

In early January 1942 I flew in Anson 3124 with pilot Flight Lieutenant Smallman to Cape Town on the last exercise of the course, and made aviation history by taking sextant readings which proved conclusively that the aircraft was flying backwards! The pilot was not amused, but then pilots never did have a sense of humour. Then came the final examinations and I well remember my navigation instructor's disapproving look when he found me in the classroom one evening entrenched behind half a dozen beer bottles carrying out some frenzied revision.

On 12 January we commenced the bombing course, still at Oudtshoorn but this time in Oxford aircraft; the course finished on 30 January after nine bombing trips. While still on this course we had a farewell dinner in the Central Hotel, Oudtshoorn, for all pupils on No. 12 Air Observers' Course. I still have the menu, on the inside of which are the signatures of my fellow pupils and the instructors. The results of our studies had been published and my logbook duly endorsed. I had not done at all badly and was by now feeling less of a stranger. Incidentally my worst marks were in wireless in which I only just passed! Things moved rapidly from here on as we were posted to No. 43 Air School, Port Alfred, for a gunnery course, and arrived on 2 February.

My impressions of No. 43 Air School are somewhat hazy as we only stayed there a fortnight. One thing stands out in my mind: the area was infested with ticks and when some of the more adventurous went for a walk through long grass they came back with their legs covered in these repulsive creatures, one or two finishing up with really nasty sores and tick fever as a result. These pests were so bad that we were instructed to report immediately to sick quarters at any time of the day or night when one was found.

By this time my logbook showed a total of 208 hours and 5 minutes' flying time and at long last I could pin up my observer's brevet, together with my sergeant's stripes. Out of the lot of us only one was commissioned, a tall pale sickly youth – or was I biased? It seemed funny to be sewing on khaki stripes, but very pleasant nevertheless. As I was still feeling a little bolshy I sewed up an air gunner's brevet on one of my tunics so that when the mood took me I could parade about as a wireless operator/air gunner among a bunch of observers, to the confusion of the permanent staff. This was very childish but underlined my resentment of the way we pupils were treated at times by the permanent staff, most of whom had not been out there as long as I had.

From 43 Air School we departed by train for a transit camp in Cape Town, where we came under the wing of an appalling South

African warrant officer whose chief aim in life seemed to be to impress upon us that although we had three stripes on each arm we were still less than nothing. This came as a great shock to me as I had been long enough in the ranks to have quite a healthy respect for a sergeant's rank, and to find that having obtained it it seemed to count for nothing was not pleasant. Later I discovered that this appeared a deliberate policy, and we met many more instances of it. Indeed, I would go so far as to say that it contributed not a little to the almost complete breakdown in Air Force discipline that I was to experience in later years. My guess is that some little man in the Air Ministry was worried about the large number of senior NCOs and officers being churned out by the Empire Air Training Scheme and took pains to emphasise the fact, which we were often told, that our rank was only a protection in the case of our being taken prisoner and did not really mean anything more.

Much to our relief our stay in the transit camp was short and we soon boarded the ship that was to take us home. Before doing this we all did some frantic shopping and each of us had at least one kitbag bulging with cigarettes, clothes, food, etc., to take back to our rationed families at home.

CHAPTER 3

Return to Britain and Final Training

The ship on which we found ourselves was an armed merchant cruiser. She had been sunk once already during the war and somebody had been stupid enough to salvage her. This fact alone emphasised to us how desperate our shipping situation must be. The deck planks were all rotten and her armament consisted of a six-inch gun on the stern and twin .5-inch water-cooled machine-guns mounted in steel towers on the boat deck. We were allocated to cabins – a pleasant change from the journey out – but before we could relax in our new found luxury we were told to move out into the aft hold and were provided with hammocks which we slung where we could. The buzz went round the ship that we were taking on refugees from Singapore, which had just fallen, so we felt that our suffering was in a good cause. Our sailing was delayed, and one day when were were all leaning over the rail impatiently waiting for them a large lorry arrived packed high with trunks and cases. This caused us some surprise as the story we had heard was that these women had literally taken the last boat out of Singapore and been seen off by their husbands who then went into captivity. Shortly afterwards the refugees arrived and to our horror each had at least three or four children of varying ages.

When all were aboard we set sail on our own. We were directly below the potato locker and it soon became evident that these had gone rotten. Before they were shovelled over the side the dirty stinking potato water had dripped through the deck over our heads and all over our kit. We had a tiny room allocated to us as a sergeants' mess and once again we were allowed the freedom of the stern. Our solitary newly commissioned officer had the full use of the boat deck!

It was a Sunday when we eventually steamed up the Clyde. I have no record of the exact date but remember it gave us all a real thrill,

13

and was a fine view of Britain at war. In every shipyard along the Clyde they were working hard building naval vessels, and as we drew alongside each yard all the men would stop work and give us a rousing cheer as we leant over the rails watching them. It was quite spontaneous and made one feel very proud to be part of such a team. We were soon put on a troop train and whisked overnight the length of the country to arrive the next day at Bournemouth.

The contrast that greeted us here was hard to understand. I was told that Bournemouth had strenuously opposed having any troops within its refined boundaries but when the pressure became too great reluctantly consented to becoming an Air Crew Reception Centre, as at least the troops would be senior NCOs or officers. We were all billeted in the large hotels on the seafront and apart from one parade each morning when literally hundreds of aircrew lined the roads to be told of the latest postings we had the rest of the day to ourselves and that, of course, meant spending our money in Bournemouth. Ice-cream was freely available, at a price, and there were numerous cafés complete with orchestras in which to while away the evening. One band I remember had as a favourite a number which began 'If you want it you gotta buy it as we ain't giving nothin' away' – and how right they were. We were issued with tickets to obtain meals from the hotel restaurants and the food was excellent.

Despite our luxury surroundings Bournemouth was, like all transit camps, a depressing place to be, and we were all glad when our posting came through to No. 9 (O)AFU (Observer) Advanced Flying Unit, Penrhos, North Wales. We arrived on 5 May 1942. No. 9 was not a happy place, and this we quickly found out. Immediately on disembarking from the train we were ordered out on to a station commander's parade, after which we were paraded outside station headquarters by the station warrant officer. In front of a few delighted airmen who happened to be passing we were given the dressing down of our lives for being so scruffy. One of our number was an ex-sergeant from a Scottish regiment who had come out from Dunkirk. With a back like a gun-barrel and craggy face set like granite he crashed out the regulation two paces forward and in a voice like gravel requested 'Permission to see the CO, SIR!' It did no good, for we found out later that this was standard procedure and was carried out on each new course to put the participants firmly in their place from the beginning. So much for the dignity of our new sergeants' stripes! Another minor irritant was the fact that on this, the first Royal Air Force station on which we had served as senior NCOs, we were forbidden the use of the sergeants' mess and had our meals in a corner of the airmen's mess separated from the rest by a piece of dirty blanket hung across the room on a length of string.

All this, however, was as nothing compared to the fact that for the first time we were going to fly in what had been operational aircraft, that is the Blenheim – both long and short nosed. We gathered round these battered, old, dirty, worn-out, oil-stained machines and gazed at them with awe. Soon we were flying in them; the pilots were all Poles and quite foolhardy. They threw those old machines about in the most incredible manner and it was on one of these occasions in the nose of a Blenheim that I was for the first and last time violently airsick. The course only lasted seventeen days, during which time we carried out map-reading exercises to get used to the terrain of this country, some air photography, bombing and air firing. No transport was ever provided round the perimeter track, nobody ever seemed to know exactly where your aircraft was and we all spent weary hours lugging cameras, navigation bags, flying kit, parachutes, etc., from one side of the aerodrome to the other until we all swore that our arms were at least three inches longer.

On 29 May we were detached to the satellite of Llandwrog for night flying in our old friends the Ansons. Our pilots were British sergeant pilots and on the whole we were glad to get away from the atmosphere of Penrhos to the more relaxed conditions of a small satellite. We only stayed until 6 June and I logged 9 hours 15 minutes' night flying, all of which was hectic, as the following incidents may show. On a cross-country navigation exercise I confidently tapped the pilot on the shoulder and told him to turn to port when he reached the coast ahead. He gave me an odd look and asked me to repeat my instructions, which I did, and finished up by pointing down at the approaching coastline. He gazed out of the aircraft for a few moments then looked at me and said sadly, 'That coastline is a cloud.' We finally got back to base without steering the last course at all!

Once again it was a parting of the ways, and strange to say I was sent on my way with an 'Above Average' assessment on my logbook. There had been ten of us on No. 14 AFU course at Penrhos; of the other nine I never saw a one again. Some were posted to Bomber Command on 'Heavies', some to Coastal Command and I to No. 17 OTU, Upwood, near Peterborough, arriving on 9 June. This meant that we had been assigned to medium daylight bombers of No. 2 Group, and I for one was very pleased.

No. 17 OTU, Upwood, was a large, well-run, pre-war aerodrome and in fact was the first 'real' RAF station that I had been on. The instructors were all operational veterans 'on rest', and we looked with awe at the liberal sprinkling of DFCs and DFMs. Most of the instructors were NCOs with the rank of flight sergeant, and the few officer instructors were flying officers with an occasional warrant officer or flight lieutenant. I remember one flight lieutenant observer with the DFC whom I regarded as the ultimate peak to be aimed at. We were formed into No. 47 Course and comprised fourteen pilots, fourteen observers and fourteen wireless operator/air gunners. We were all sergeants apart from five of the pilots who were commissioned officers. At the time of closing my logbook I had noted that over half had been killed to my knowledge.

At the beginning of the course the pilots, observers and air gunners all attended separate instruction and we found ourselves back in Ansons carrying out photography, map reading and dead reckoning navigation in B Flight; this lasted until 4 July.

We were now brought together to attend lectures as a course. Among the pilots were five officers as I have mentioned: one was a South American, very nice but rather older than the rest of us, one was a brawny Scot, one a very handsome young Englishman, one an old (at least thirty-five!) flight lieutenant ex-Training Command instructor regarded with awe by us all and left well alone (he was subsequently shot down on his first operational trip and the story was that he was such a good pilot that he could not bring himself to take evasive action and throw the aircraft about), and the fifth a six foot two Canadian. The last of these, Dick, and I used to sit together at lectures, at which he used always to fall fast asleep, relying on me to give him a nudge when necessary. The forming of crews was left entirely to ourselves. First the pilots and observers teamed up, and Dick and I decided to make a go of it; as I was an ex-wireless operator he left it to me to pick a wireless operator/air gunner. My choice was a shy, serious, stocky Yorkshireman called Frank, with close-cropped head and steel-rimmed spectacles. I have since bitterly regretted this decision many times as I became very fond of Frank and it turned out to be virtually a death sentence for him.

We were now moved to C Flight at Upwood and on 12 July, I flew for the first time with my new pilot, Pilot Officer Dick Christie, in Blenheim Mk IV No. 5741. On the way out to the aircraft my pilot suddenly stopped and said to me 'Have I got to sign something first?' and it dawned on me that he knew as little about flying as I did about navigation and bombing. This was further demonstrated when, after having strapped ourselves in, Pilot Officer Christie tested the engines, throttled back and called for a mechanic. The mechanic leaned into the cockpit and made no bones about pointing out that the propeller pitch levers were incorrectly set. Poor old Dick turned a bright scarlet and off we went. The bombing range for which we were heading was only about five miles away but all my worries about my pilot's flying ability were quickly dispelled because for the first time I was also on my own as navigator and it took immense effort on my part to find the place, despite the three huge chimneys conveniently situated nearby. Returning to the aerodrome was also a worrying business so I was in no mood to criticise the extremely bumpy landing. Our air gunner, Frank Swainson, was waiting for me when we landed and was very anxious to know what sort of a pilot we had. I was too shaken by the whole experience to quibble so I said 'Fine', and he appeared satisfied. Looking back on it I would say that was the most dangerous flight that I ever made. Later Dick told me that, back in Canada, he nearly had not become a pilot. On his first solo flight he decided to give his home town, which was nearby, a buzz. Apparently the local police sergeant got on the telephone to his CO and reported him. As evidence he said into the telephone, 'Here he comes again, Sir', and stuck the telephone out of the window. The sound which filled the CO's ears left him in no doubt about the height at which Dick was flying.

On 14 July we took off in Blenheim 5876 as a crew for the very first time. Once again we visited the nearby bombing range, which I found with a little less difficulty, and then back to Upwood for another very bumpy landing. When we rolled to a stop there was silence in the aircraft, and Dick sat there very red in the face. Suddenly a voice from the gun turret at the back said 'Any more of that and I'll remuster as a ruddy grasshopper'. The tension was broken and from that moment I think we became a crew.

On 31 July we moved to D Flight for more bombing practice, and on 6 August I made my one and only night flight from Upwood in an Anson; needless to say it was disastrous! The flight consisted of a cross-country navigational exercise followed by a bombing run on a nearby range, and finished with another cross-country navigational exercise. The first cross-country passed without incident and then we arrived at the night bombing range. This consisted of a circle of white lights shining up out of the darkness of wartime Britain. The old Anson did not have any intercommunication system and the method of guiding the pilot to the target was crude in the extreme. One pupil lay on his stomach in the nose gazing down into the blackness through an open hatch into which the cold night air roared into his face, and the other pupil sat on a seat behind him and held one of his feet in either hand. To direct the pilot to turn left the first pupil raised his left leg which was felt by the second pupil who then yelled in the pilot's ear 'Turn left!' To stop the turn the first pupil put his leg down and the second pupil told the pilot to level out, and so on. In addition, the second pupil operated the bomb doors. To do this he unclipped a handle on his right-hand side and wound the doors open or shut as the case may be. On this particular night my fellow pupil asked me to drop his eight bombs in addition to my own, and just before getting down into the nose our sergeant pilot told me in a morose manner that I had better drop each bomb first as he was not blankety well going round a second time!

After a certain amount of leg waving the target hove in sight and at what I hoped was the right moment I pressed the bomb button. Peering out into the darkness I waited to see the results but nothing apparently happened, and by this time the pilot had banked round and was beginning the second run-up, so with more leg waggling we dropped the second bomb and once again I could not see any result. This procedure was carried out until all sixteen bombs had gone. By this time I was very stiff and frozen to the marrow, and convinced that my night vision was even worse than I had thought. Our pilot left the range and started off on the first course of our second cross-country navigational exercise. I thankfully closed the trapdoor and climbed out of the nose and sat beside the pilot. After a few minutes I leaned over to the other pupil navigator and asked him if he had closed the bomb doors. He gave me a strange look and said no, so I bent down and undid the clip holding the bomb door handle – upon which it immediately leapt out of my grasp and spun round giving me a severe rap over the knuckles in the process. Seconds afterwards there was a violent explosion just below the aircraft and the sky lit up with a vivid flash. Our pilot nearly jumped out of his skin and asked 'What the X Y Z was that?' Looking down below and astern I perceived there was a fair-sized fire burning on the ground and I suddenly went cold as I realised what had happened. The bomb doors must never have been opened and I had cheerfully dropped all sixteen bombs on to them. The weight of the bombs on the doors had forced them open as soon as I had released the handle from its clip, and away all sixteen had gone. Some must have hit each other on the way down which would account for the violent explosion; as for the destination of the remainder I preferred not to speculate so quietly closed the bomb doors.

The second exercise passed without incident until we returned to base to find that the aerodrome lights had been extinguished. We cruised around the marker beacon which was situated as usual a few miles away. After half an hour of this we received a coded wireless message from base which we decoded with difficulty. It said simply 'There is an Air Raid in Progress'. By now we were getting very short of petrol so we carried out all the distress procedures in which we had so recently been trained – nothing happened. Soon I saw what appeared to be the lights of an aerodrome and excitedly pointed them out to our pilot who only made rude remarks to the effect that he had landed on a dummy aerodrome a month before and was not going to repeat the performance. (These dummy aerodromes were deliberately illuminated during an air raid to encourage the Germans to bomb them, and apparently our pilot had not only crashed on one but had suffered the indignity of being bombed afterwards.) By now our situation was really serious. All the petrol gauges were showing zero and there was not a light to be seen anywhere. Remembering my South African days and the power of an Aldis signalling lamp on a lonely tramp steamer I crawled to the back of the Anson, got out the Aldis lamp and flashed out into the inky darkness the letters SOS. This was definitely not in the instruction manual but the result was most gratifying. Immediately on our port the lights of a large aerodrome blazed on and our pilot hurriedly banked towards them. On the approach our starboard engine cut out through lack of fuel but we pressed firmly downwards towards mother earth and at long last felt the wheels touch the ground. Before we had finished our run two things happened: the lights were all turned off, plunging the world back into darkness, and our port engine cut out as its fuel supply ran dry! We rolled to a stop in total darkness and sat back thankfully waiting for help to arrive. We sat and we sat and nothing happened so I volunteered to go and look for someone and set off down the runway back in the direction from which we had just come.

After a while I came to the caravan which is always situated at the approach end of the runway and there was a sergeant leaning against the side of the vehicle smoking and gazing idly up at the night sky. 'Hello', I said. 'Hello', he replied; then after a pause casually, 'Were you in that aircraft that just landed?' By now I was filled with a righteous indignation brought on no doubt by relief at our near escape, and asked him sarcastically if that was how they always treated shot-up aircraft landing full of wounded men. The idea clearly startled him and I soon had transport laid on to collect the rest of the crew. We spent an unpleasant night sleeping in our clothes and an even more unpleasant time next morning starting up the old Anson by hand-cranking after it had been refuelled, then back we went to base and the incident of the bombing range was now fainter in my mind. Two days later it became fainter still when I saw the bombing results of that memorable night on the notice-board. My fellow pupil and I had, it seemed, done very well. Fate, however, caught up with us, for a week later I was called into the CO's presence and asked whether I had observed the results of my night bombing. I shifted my feet and mumbled 'No', whereupon the story came out. Apparently our bombs had landed smack on top of a prominent country farmer's biggest barn, and the resulting fire had needed the attention of four local brigades. The next morning the farmer was mournfully looking over the results of what he thought was enemy action when he came across a fragment of metal with 'Made in Birmingham' stamped on it. In the middle of a world war with enemy aircraft all over the place our dear old Air Ministry just had to be so efficient that they traced the culprits. Yet the mystery of our non-existent bombing results was never explained, and strange to say I never heard another thing about the incident.

Shortly after this a strange aircraft landed at Upwood and when it came to rest at dispersal we all grouped around. It was a Boston

Mk III with which some squadrons had just been equipped. Standing on its tricycle undercarriage it looked very odd to us, with its narrow fuselage and big tail. On investigating the observer's position I saw that it consisted of a small compartment right in the nose, surrounded by windows and with an armour-plated bulkhead cutting it off from the rest of the crew. This did not appeal to me at all and I declared to all and sundry that I did not want to be posted to a Boston squadron. Air Ministry must have heard me. We were posted to a Boston squadron.

On 14 August 1942 we took off on our last cross-country in Blenheim No. 9305 on what must have been one of the most dangerous flights of my career. We had to fly north from Upwood then east out into the North Sea and back south-west down to Norfolk and base. A simple enough job one would think – but not for such raw crews as us.

Shortly after take-off we ran into thick cloud, and after a while I became worried as to our position so asked my pilot to descend so that I could see the ground. Down, down, down we went, until suddenly we broke cloud a few feet above the ground, which luckily for us was flat. I go hot and cold all over every time I think of that light-hearted descent. Nothing daunted, we flew on until the time came to turn out and fly over the North Sea. A Spitfire came up and flew alongside us, the pilot giving us a very hard look as these were the days when all sorts of rumours abounded about British aircraft being used by the Germans. I switched my microphone on and commented to the crew on how silly the Spitfire pilot was to come so close as we could easily shoot him down. 'Yes', said the voice of our air gunner, 'But what about the one just under our tail?'

On 19 August we made our last flight from Upwood in Blenheim No. 9375 and dropped our first live 250 lb GP bombs in the mud flats in the Wash. When the postings were announced we saw that we were destined for No. 226 Squadron, Swanton Morley, Norfolk. We arrived on 30 August, by which time my logbook had recorded 273 hours 30 minutes' day flying and 17 hours 5 minutes' night flying.

CHAPTER 4

No. 226 Squadron – Bostons – 1942

Swanton Morley was a peacetime RAF station and had good
permanent buildings set in the quiet and lovely Norfolk
countryside some five miles north of the little market town of
Dereham. It had a grass landing-field and a friendly intimate
atmosphere. At the time of our arrival No. 226 Squadron was the
only operational squadron on the station, the only other occupants
being a Beam Approach Training Flight of Oxfords. Being a light
bomber squadron neither the officers' nor sergeants' mess was
crowded as each aircraft carried a crew of only three. We learned
that No. 226 Squadron had only fairly recently been equipped with
Bostons and previously had used the Blenheim Mk IV with which
they had carried out many raids on enemy coastal shipping. These
attacks had been so costly that the squadron had been sent to
Northern Ireland to rest and re-equip and had only just returned
to operational duty. We were told by the old-timers that there must
be a wall of Blenheims lying on the sea-bed just off the Dutch
coast. We were posted to B Flight and our flight commander was a
red-haired squadron leader called Kennedy who was an ace flyer
and very popular; we regarded him with awe. We little realised
then that we were a replacement crew for one of those lost by the
squadron during smoke-laying during the Dieppe operations.

We had our first flight together as a crew on 4 September, in
Boston III AL750, and for the next fortnight flew hard on cross-
country, formation and bombing trips. My dislike of the Boston
rapidly disappeared and I revelled in the unrivalled view I had from
the nose. We had arrived on the squadron at a bad time; the previous
week one of the crews had hit a telegraph pole on a low-level flight
and damaged the nosewheel so that on landing it had collapsed and

the navigator had been dragged along the ground on what was left of his legs. He died shortly afterwards. On our first low-level we were hopping across the fields when I spied a very tall poplar tree ahead. Dick started to pull up but it was obvious that he had left it too late. I saw the top of the tree coming closer and closer then BASH! – and my two-inch-thick bullet-proof bombing panel shattered, letting in a tornado of twigs and leaves. My map wrapped itself around my face and above the din I heard the very shaky voice of my pilot asking if I were all right. For the life of me I dared not try to waggle my toes but removed the map from my face and gazed down. Much to my relief my legs were still there. We made a safe landing back at base, and luckily I never had to complain of such treatment again.

It soon became apparent to Frank and me that we had a good pilot and we all worked hard to become a good crew. As I have said the Boston was a lovely aircraft to fly in but because of the fact that each member of the crew was in a separate compartment and could only speak to each other through the intercom snags developed. I had a bad tendency in the early days to steal Frank's thunder. Dick would ask him to get a radio bearing and as soon as it came through I would hear it on the intercom and give it to Dick while Frank was busy acknowledging the message. As soon as I realised that this was getting under Frank's skin I kept quiet. We found that it was an advantage to have a pilot who was also an officer as in those days very few squadron pilots were commissioned. Being in the officers' mess was a distinct advantage, as he was always able to get us extra flights and he was 'in the know' as to what was going on. Dick was not in the least interested in navigation; he never worried his head about where we were and concentrated on flying the aircraft. I took this as a compliment and tried my best never to let him down by getting lost.

Most of our practice flying was in formation. We used to fly in a 'box' of six aircraft made up of two V-formations of three aircraft each, with the leader of the second V slightly below the first. New crews were detailed to fly in the tailend charlie positions at the back of the second V because any poor flying on their part would not split up the formation. The squadron prided itself on very tight formation flying, and we used literally to tuck our wing into the space between our leader's wing and tail.

On 15 September in Boston AL670 we carried out a sea-sweep. These operations were not very popular as they consisted of flying at wave-top height in formation out to a point very near the enemy coast, then climbing to 500 feet and patrolling a given area, keeping in line abreast about half a mile apart, looking for some poor unfortunates who had come down in the sea. The trips were also unpopular because they only counted as half an operation; because we often mysteriously lost an aircraft always on one of the flanks; and because despite weary peering at the waves we never saw anything. At this stage of the war a tour of daylight operations was counted as twenty. Nobody had done that many to my knowledge but a few lucky crews had got through fifteen and gone for a well-deserved 'rest'.

On 26 September Dick and I were flown to Hooton Park to collect a Boston which was urgently required for an operation the next day from the maintenance unit there. We were met with an air of complete indifference and told that it was not ready, so we both went to my home in Birkenhead for a spot of unexpected leave. We rang Hooton Park at frequent intervals the next day only to be told that the aircraft was still not ready. The following morning we rang up again to be told that we had better hurry as the aircraft would soon be leaving. This puzzled us, but when we arrived post-haste at Hooton Park our bewilderment turned to anger when we were informed that a ferry pilot from Ferry Command was arriving from the south of England to fly the Boston to Swanton and we would have to travel as passengers. Some kind person had discovered a regulation which said that only ferry pilots could fly aircraft from maintenance units to squadrons. In due course an Anson arrived and Dick's face was a picture when the ferry pilot cheerfully admitted that he had never flown a Boston before. He did not have a flying helmet so Dick and I had to bundle into the air gunner's compartment in the rear without any form of communication with the pilot. He made a ropey take-off and flew along with about 15° of starboard flap left down, which Dick kept looking at with deep disgust. The weather got steadily worse and in the Midlands we heard the undercarriage come down and we landed. The ferry pilot claimed that the weather was too bad to continue and disappeared in the direction of the nearest town, leaving two very disgruntled operational aircrew on a strange airfield with one operational Boston.

Dick and I held a council of war and then Dick rang our squadron commander and requested permission to bring the Boston home. This was granted and we took off, making Swanton Morley half an hour later. I have often wondered what that ferry pilot thought when he turned up next morning to find the Boston gone.

It was on this trip that we gained an insight into the workings of the official mind behind the fighting man. We knew that our engineering officer had been complaining ever since the squadron had re-equipped with Bostons that he had no official maintenance manuals, and were staggered to find that each Boston that arrived in Britain had a copy of the most lavish maintenance instructions printed in the usual American style. These, together with sundry other fittings such as thermos flasks for each crew member, were taken out at the maintenance unit and they had hangars full of them as they were not on the Air Ministry lists of equipment required!

By the end of September we had completed 26 hours 20 minutes' flying on an operational squadron. October started with more practice flying and we dropped 'smoke' for the first time on the bombing range. Everybody was aware that Britain held stocks of gas bombs but this was never referred to and we only exercised with smoke-bombs and smoke-canisters that sprayed out a dense white cloud underneath the aircraft. About this time we put our heads together as a crew and discussed what we would do in the event of Dick, our pilot, being wounded in action. As already mentioned there was no communication between the observer and pilot other than the intercom and a small flashing light. The situation was similar between the pilot and air gunner but in their case they also had a clip on a wire running between pulley-wheels that could take a message between them. Strange to relate there was a control column which could be affixed in the air gunner's compartment, but no instruments! As we felt reluctant to advocate our baling out and leaving a wounded pilot to his fate we devised a system whereby WOp/AG Frank flew the plane from the rear (he could not see ahead, incidentally) and I gave him directions from the nose using my instruments. We got quite good at it under Dick's patient tuition and reached the stage where we reckoned that we could have landed the plane between us even though it would have had to be a full wheels-up affair. Fate was, however, to decree otherwise and make a cruel mockery of all our puny efforts.

By now we had settled down to squadron life and become reasonably efficient; there remained only the ordeal by fire. We had a large crew-room in one of the hangars just behind the control tower; it had the usual notices and maps on the walls, and easy chairs all round with a sizeable table in the middle over which was suspended a very large model of a He111 covered in dust. Between practice flights we used to hang about this room and, if the weather was fine, could play at throwing horseshoes at an iron stake on the grass outside. The flight commanders had their offices nearby. Some aircrew could relax easily, some not. The senior crews were a pleasant lot but held themselves somewhat aloof from the raw recruits. All in all we must have been at our highest pitch of enthusiasm at this time.

At this stage of the war we were living in an old country mansion about five miles from the airfield, as the RAF still retained bitter memories of the aircrew killed during the bombing of the Battle of Britain fighter stations. It was an eerie semi-derelict old place with an antiquated lighting system of its own; naked bulbs emitted a feeble yellow light in the bare rooms equipped only with iron service bedsteads. (Later in the war it was taken over as a Group Headquarters and of course no money was spared on repairs for the chairborne warriors.) We slept in one room as a crew. I well remember the briefing for our first operation which was to take place the next day. I lay awake long into the night and the restless tossing and turning of the other occupants of the room told their own story.

So it was, on 17 October, we found ourselves on the Battle Order for the first time. At 1400 hours, fully briefed and dressed the part, we took off in Boston AL278 for a 'Circus' on the docks at Le Havre. At 1508 we were recalled to base.

The reason for our recall was an interesting one. We had been briefed to fly at low level over the mouth of the Thames on our way south to the rendezvous with the fighters at Beachy Head. Our track crossed over the town of Southend on the north bank of the Thames and we had been assured that their balloon barrage would be close-hauled, but were told to watch out for any balloons flying from ships entering or leaving the river which would not have been alerted. It was a very hazy day with poor visibility and as we were approaching Southend I warned Dick that we were coming to the river. Suddenly I saw a large silvery shape looming up well above us – a barrage balloon! The formation split up in all directions and I had a quick glimpse of bomb-laden Bostons standing on one wing trip as they dodged cables before all was blotted out by the mist. As we were flying tailend charlie Dick had time to open the throttles wide and attempt to climb above the barrage. Our nose was pointing straight at a balloon and it loomed larger and larger out of the mist. I unclipped the Browning machine-gun and aimed at the monster, thinking that if I shot it down we would be all right, but in a moment's reflection I realised that when it caught fire we would be caught in the flames as we were so close. Luckily, we just scraped over the top of it and emerged into clear sky with no other aircraft in sight. When we got back to base we found that there was one aircraft missing. He turned up some twenty minutes later, very white faced and shaken. What had upset him was not flying through the barrage but the fact that he had rashly gone on to the rendezvous with the fighters, and had almost to fight his way out from one hundred and fifty Spitfires which were all set to escort him on his own across the Channel.

At this time the squadron were employed on two types of operations. The first was called a 'Circus' and consisted of twelve or at the most eighteen Bostons. We would take off in pairs and form into a tight box before the first planes airborne had completed a circuit, then over the airfield in nice formation at 0 feet and set course to some prominent landmark on the south coast, such as Selsey Bill or Beachy Head, still at low level. We had to meet our fighter escort at this point and so critical was their petrol consumption that we were only allowed plus or minus half a minute either way of the rendezvous time, otherwise the fighters had to return to their bases. We used to fly straight out to sea at 0 feet and the fighters formed up around us as we set course. It was a grand sight. Ten minutes before reaching the enemy coast, at a point always referred to as position A, we would start climbing so that we crossed the enemy coast at 10,000 feet. In theory this gave the enemy the least possible time to detect us on their radar. Circus operations usually targeted docks or some bridge only a very short distance from the coast, the main idea being to bring the German fighters into combat – and we were the bait! The bombing run, which had to be made with the formation flying straight and level, was the most dangerous point as regards ack-ack fire, and it was a tribute to the accuracy of the German anti-aircraft guns that twenty seconds was considered to be the longest time that could be taken without getting the whole formation peppered. After the bombing run a left-hand diving turn for home, and back at 0 feet. The Spitfires used to get very niggled if we dived too steeply because they would then fall behind us as they had to 'weave' continually to watch their tails. Needless to say these operations required a clear sky as bombing targets were always picked out visually.

The second type of operation consisted of low-level individual attacks on such targets as power stations, generally some ten minutes' flying time from the coast. This was, of course, without fighter cover.

At most six Bostons would set out to attack three targets, two aircraft to each target, the second aircraft flying on exactly the same course as the first but two minutes behind. These flights were made at 0 feet with the exception of crossing the enemy coast which had to be done in cloud; the cloud base had to be no higher than 1,500 feet and had to stretch to the target so that use could be made of it in the event of being 'jumped' by enemy fighters. So many aircraft had been lost by misjudging the height of the cloud base that we had to make a check half-way across the Channel. These operations, we had been told at Upwood, were a 'piece of cake' as we flew so low the Germans were taken by surprise and even when they saw us they could not swing their guns round in time.

On 26 October we took off in Boston Z2116 to have another go at Le Havre but once again were forced to return because of bad weather. Five days later we took off in Boston AL748 at 1115 hours as the second aircraft on a low-level attack on the power station at Mazingarbe in France.

To receive the news that you are to take part in an operation is a peculiar experience. It can come by seeing your name on the Battle Order in the mess, or when walking round the perimeter track with your friends by the impersonal voice of the Tannoy. From then on you are a being apart; your steps are taking you down a very different path from those around you, perhaps to your death. Death was a word I never heard spoken on a squadron. Old So-and-So had 'gone for a Burton', 'gone for a loop' or had 'bought it', but never died. However, it was death and the imminent possibility of death that in a strange way made squadron life so magnetically attractive.

At the appointed time crews would be seen converging on the operations room, which was an underground bunker near the main gates. Navigators would be carrying a large green canvas satchel full of maps and the tools of their trade. Inside the operations room would be an air of tension. By the door, standing behind small tables, stood the members of the Intelligence staff ready to hand out to each crew member an escape kit, a bar of chocolate and a packet of chewing gum, together with a small bag into which you emptied the contents of your pockets for safe keeping and to ensure that you did not carry any useful documents in the event of being taken prisoner. Navigators were, in my opinion, the lucky ones because, after briefing by the various specialists, they had a busy time drawing in the tracks on their maps and working out the courses to steer to and from the target. The pilots and WOp/AGs had more time on their hands during which to worry. Being a Canadian my pilot was very fond of gum; being greedy I was very fond of chocolate. We always did a profitable swap and I always made myself slightly sick gobbling chocolate on the way out to the target – just in case!

In the operations room watches were synchronised and all times set: time of start-up, time of taxi out, time of take-off, etc. The senior officer leading the attack would climb up on to the platform and give us a brief outline of the tactics required, to be followed by the various experts such as the meteorological officer, intelligence officer, gunnery officer, etc. If it was an important trip the station commander himself would get up and give us all a little pep-talk. From the operations room a bus would take us to the locker room and we would collect our flying kit. As the Boston was a well-heated aircraft we used to fly in battle dress, flying boots and helmets – only the air gunners put on their heavy fur-lined Irvine jackets. On this particular low-level attack on the power station at Mazingarbe I remember that Frank was worried, as we should have been going on leave that day; he asked one of his friends who was not on the operation if he would send a telegram to his wife telling her that he would be late. This would have to be done well after we were on our way back from the target as the aerodrome was always sealed off from the outside world before an operation took place. Back into the crew bus we climbed, complete with parachutes and gear, six crews, eighteen men, all knowing that the average losses on such an operation were two crews, six men – a one in three chance.

Navigation at low level in those days was done entirely by map reading and taking drifts over the sea and was a difficult business, as a high degree of accuracy was called for in order to avoid the heavily defended areas. An error of a quarter of a mile off-course could be, and often was, fatal. Understandably I was very anxious to make a success of this, my first, low-level operation and as we thundered across the Channel just above the wave tops I wondered, in my lonely seat in the nose, whether we were on track. Just before we reached the enemy coast we climbed up into cloud, which was just at the right height of 1,500 feet, and weaved about in it as we crossed into enemy territory for the first time. When I told Dick to break cloud and get back down to ground level I looked anxiously ahead and was overjoyed to see a fleeting glimpse of another Boston far ahead. It was our flight commander, which meant that we were on course. Fields and hedges flashed by beneath the nose; for the first time I was looking at occupied France. Dick was flying superbly. Suddenly we flashed past lines of French workers cycling home to lunch (whenever possible, attacks were made during lunch hours to reduce the casualties among French workers), and they waved to us like mad. I waved back feeling very proud and thinking of all the heroic war films I had ever seen.

I was still waving when it started. It sounded as though somebody had a big stick and was beating it against the sides of the aircraft so that it seemed very loud, even above the bellow of the two sturdy Pratt and Whitney radial engines pulling us along at some 260 m.p.h. Looking around all I could see were guns and gun-pits and streams of tracer shells floating lazily upwards then whizzing suddenly past. The noise of the engines slackened, our speed dropped, and to my surprise we started to climb, making ourselves a perfect target. There was a sound just behind me as loud as a pistol shot, and the aircraft shuddered. I switched on my microphone to speak to Dick but it was dead. I frantically tore the plug out and put it in the emergency socket, but that was dead too.

The Boston was now flying straight and level and we were making no attempt to take evasive action; our airspeed had dropped to 180 m.p.h., the dreadful thump, thump, thump continued on the fuselage. Had Dick climbed to this height so that we could bale out? No, we were only at 500 feet – no parachute could be guaranteed to open at that height. Was Dick wounded? I did not know: I was trapped in a Perspex walled space six feet long by four feet wide by five feet high with my back against an armour-plated bulkhead, and I could not get in touch with any other member of the crew to find out what was going on. After what seemed like an age the thumping and the tracer stopped and we slowly lost height. Another fear seized me: were we going to crash-land? If so I stood no chance at all, but the good old Boston kept going until, incredibly, I saw the power station at Mazingarbe loom up ahead. I reached for the bomb release button – strange to say the Americans had so fitted the Boston out that the pilot had the controls for opening and shutting the bomb doors – and as we roared over the roof I gave a hearty press. We did a climbing turn up towards the safety of the clouds and as I looked back at the target I noticed that it was enveloped in smoke, so noted the time in my log and also entered 'Hits seen'. I observed too that they were shooting at us and felt indignant, as Intelligence had assured us that the target was undefended. My automatic camera, which should have started taking film when I pressed the bomb release, had not functioned so I switched it on by hand; then none too soon we were swallowed up in cloud.

My feeling of relief soon gave way to dismay when I realised that I could not give my pilot a course for base, and knowing Dick's complete lack of interest in this subject I knew that he would not have the faintest idea. This was borne out when I checked my compass and saw the course that we were steering. We were wandering north over France. Eventually Dick decided to come down out of the clouds to see what was below. Of all places he chose Ostend, one of the most heavily defended Channel ports, and they lived up to their reputation by giving us a thoroughly unpleasant reception. Dick, however, had seen the sea and he dived down to wave-top height and headed away from the land. For the first time I began to relax and on looking around was rather puzzled to see the huge columns of water that suddenly sprang up around us until I realised that the six-inch shore batteries were shooting at us! We were soon out of range and I thought that our troubles were over until it dawned on me that our course would take us right up the middle of the North Sea until we ran out of petrol. There followed a painful period in which I nearly flattened my tin hat on the armour-plated bulkhead in a futile endeavour to attract Dick's attention. (We carried tin hats on low-level raids as a protection against shell splinters coming in through the top of the aircraft, but many crews openly admitted to sitting on them in times of stress to protect more vital parts.)

Eventually I calmed down and hit on the idea of sending a message in Morse on the emergency light to Frank in the rear so that he could write it out and wind it forward to Dick on the emergency pulley system. Many attempts failed until I got a very shaky reply requesting 'Course'. From this I presumed that Frank was injured as the Morse was so poor. I sent out the course very slowly over and over again and was much relieved when we swung slowly to port and headed for home. We crossed the Norfolk coast to the accompaniment of only poor shooting by our own defences, and just as I hoped that all was now well Dick sighted another Boston and swung away to take up formation alongside it. This aircraft took no notice of us and proceeded untroubled out to sea over the Wash, no doubt on a routine navigational exercise. Seeing the sea below us Dick turned around and headed back inland, missing our base and circling Watton, a big RAF station about twenty miles from Swanton Morley. From my position in the nose I could just see the ends of the wings and by the state of them we were in a bad way, so I was very relieved when I heard the landing wheels bang down. We came in to land very fast and seemed to float a long way, not touching down until we were over half-way down the runway. No brakes were applied and we carried on at high speed across the perimeter track and down into a dispersal. I stayed where I was for the simple reason that to jump out of my bottom hatch would have meant being chopped up by one or other of the propellers. With great presence of mind Dick opened up one engine to full throttle and thanks to the robust undercarriage of the Boston we skidded right round and headed back the way we came, narrowly missing a truck which was going round the perimeter track. Once Dick had the aircraft under control we taxied up to the control tower and he switched off the engines. I was in such a hurry to get out of my bottom hatch that I forgot to undo the line attached to my seat pack dinghy with the result that when I jumped out the dinghy followed me and landed on my head! Strolling casually towards me were three airmen, hands in pockets; the leading one called out, 'What did it, Sarge, flak or fighters?' For the first time I looked back at our Boston. It was in tatters, holes everywhere, but what caught my eye was the rounded belly of the aircraft from which dripped a mixture of blood and oil. I spun round and told them to get an ambulance, using true RAF vocabulary which was so effective that they disappeared in haste. Going round the wing I saw Dick raise his cockpit canopy and I called up to ask if he was all right; he said yes but told me to go and look at Frank. I tried to open the under-hatch to Frank's compartment but it was jammed. Suddenly Dick called out not to bother and as I came from underneath the aircraft Dick fell some seven feet off the wing on top of me. He had looked into Frank's shattered compartment and the sight had been too much for him. Poor Frank had received a direct hit in the head from a Bofors shell, his guns had been blown from their mountings and bits of skin, bone, blood and hair had been plastered by the slipstream all over the rear of the aircraft. The time was 1320. It had all happened in two hours and five minutes.

In a daze I was taken to the sergeants' mess for a meal, and Dick went to the officers' mess. I don't know about Dick but I did not eat a thing. The sight of that plateful of food with a thick skin on the gravy stayed with me for a long time. Eventually a Boston landed from Swanton Morley, piloted by our flight commander, and we bundled all our kit in and flew back to base. This was the first time that I had had a chance to speak to Dick and I remarked that anyway we had hit the target because I had checked the bomb bay and verified that it was empty when we landed. At this he looked more miserable than ever and said in a low voice that we had not, as he had not been able to open the bomb doors and had jettisoned the bombs in the North Sea on the way home. When we landed at Swanton Morley I remember walking to the briefing room to the accompaniment of many stares and for the first time became aware of that curious feeling, the feeling that only a survivor can have.

On returning to the sergeants' quarters I received a tremendous shock. The bed and locker next to mine belonged to Frank but to my astonishment I saw another WOp/AG sitting on the bed with his kit in Frank's locker. The speed with which all traces of Frank had been swept efficiently away and another piece of cannon-fodder put in his place was so cold-blooded that I was filled with a burning resentment, most of which I directed upon the surprised newcomer. This was my first real introduction to an aspect of squadron life which I suppose was very necessary: the insistence of all concerned on living in the present and not looking back. The only thing that refused to obey this rule was one's mind which, as time passed, became increasingly filled by the 'Ghosts' of those who had gone. They were never mentioned, no record was evident of their ever having existed, but they were there, and they would always be there in the minds of those who were left.

Later I found that the cause of our misfortune had been an enemy airfield right on our track which Intelligence had not known about. Our flight commander had taken it unawares and had a jolly time spraying all and sundry with his four fixed front machine-guns, hence their annoyance at our appearance two minutes later. The reason that Dick had throttled back and we had climbed was that the trimming controls had been shot away leaving the aircraft tail-heavy, so that it was only by throttling right back and using his not inconsiderable strength to keep the stick pushed forward that we were able to keep flying. In fact by the time we landed Dick's arms were quite numb from the continuous strain of keeping the nose down.

Dick attended Frank's funeral as he had spent a leave with Frank and his family, and he found out that Frank's wife had received the Air Ministry telegram notifying her of his death with well-practised speed, but that this was most unfortunately followed up by the telegram from Frank saying that he would be delayed. This, of course, was the telegram that Frank had asked a friend to send just before take-off.

I did not fly again until 16 November on a practice low-level cross-country and as Dick and I did not now have a complete crew I spent the rest of the month as a spare navigator flying with various other pilots on exercises. This was a miserable and depressing time; we had started off with such high hopes and had gradually become a team of which we all felt justifiably proud, and now on our first operation the team was no more. The gloom was only partially lifted by a write-up of our efforts in Group Routine Orders under the heading 'Notable War Services'.

It was on 6 December 1942 that No. 2 Group mounted a daring and large-scale daylight raid against the Philips radio works at Eindhoven in Holland. Although we had trained for it the fact that we had lost Frank meant that we were not able to take part. It was a low-level attack by ninety-three aircraft and the results were very good. Losses were mostly caused by fighters. Some crews brought back excellent photographs taken at roof-top level and all spoke of the bravery of one particular German gun crew mounted on the roof of the factory who continued to fire until engulfed in flames. Our flight commander brought back a seagull's head which had become embedded in his wing, and a photograph of him holding it was in most of the national papers. With all the talk today about the American daylight offensive it is a pity nobody seems to remember this effort on which a lot of good men died, including our station navigation officer, but the convenient legend has grown up: the RAF bombed at night and the Americans by day. Perhaps somebody, some day, will write a book about the activities of No. 2 Group, RAF, that sets the secord straight.

December opened with the same pattern of casual flights with squadron pilots who were short of an observer. On 11 December I flew to Hurn on the south coast with Flying Officer Billy Grey as pilot. He was a short Canadian with a slow drawl and a charming manner, and as deputy flight commander was in charge of the three aircraft which were carrying out the smoke-laying exercise near Bournemouth for the benefit of the Army top brass. As the exercise called for a run-in to the selected target at low level over the coast we requested clearance from coastal ack-ack, but this was refused. Fighter Command had to put up a standing patrol over that sector and Ack-Ack Command were stood down. Even so, when the day arrived we approached the cliffs with some trepidation, and sure enough the gunners had us well in their sights. Luckily for us they did not open up. The day was one of absolutely no wind and after the first few aircraft had laid smoke it hung in a great cloud over the target, so Ground Control attempted to call off our second run, but we were not to be done out of our fun and roared in through the white clouds to add more. By the time we had finished half of Bournemouth had disappeared and I am sure the top brass must have done a bit of coughing!

We had an evening or two in Bournemouth which was still packed with aircrew who had just returned from the Empire Air Training Scheme and we had a fine time shooting incredible lines to a gullible audience. One of our observers, a small wiry New Zealander, nearly swallowed his beer mug in wrath one night when he was told in all seriousness that as an observer he stood a good chance of being posted to an Advanced Training Unit soon! We were a cocky lot and delighted in the interest our unusual aircraft aroused, with their big tails sticking up in the air and their tricycle undercarriage. We delighted in taking maximum advantage of this undercarriage both for taxiing at great speed and for retracting it very quickly after take-off in the manner of the fighter boys. Sitting in the nose of an operational Boston as you taxied at speed, one after the other, past rows of staring faces on a strange aerodrome, gave you as good a feeling as being in a Lord Mayor's Parade.

On 20 December a Boston landed at Hurn piloted by Dick. He had come to collect me – we were 'On ops' the next day and we had been given a new WOp/AG, a flight sergeant called Len. Imagine my feelings when, in the operations room at Swanton Morley the following day, I learned that we had been detailed for a low-level attack on the power station at Ghent! I aired my views on this type of operation in no uncertain fashion, and my audience must have taken more notice than I supposed. While I was drawing in the tracks to the target on my maps Dick came over to me and started cutting the sergeant's stripes off my sleeve. When I protested he told me to shut up and pinned an old piece of his own pilot officer's braid on my shoulder epaulette. In this manner I discovered that I had been granted a commission, truly 'In the field'.

We took off at 1135 hours, once again as the second aircraft of a pair of two but this time Dick was in full agreement with me that, come what may, we would not be two minutes behind the leader! Across the North Sea we raced, pushing the sturdy Pratt and Whitney radials as hard as we dared. The Boston was remarkable in the fact that there was not much difference between its cruising speed of 240 m.p.h. and its maximum of 265 m.p.h. This sea crossing was much longer than the one we had made across the Channel and when the flat enemy coast loomed ahead we climbed up for cloud cover, and to my amazement I saw that we were one of a line of six Bostons all with the same idea not to be last over the target! Flying in cloud is a funny business and without instruments you lose all sense of which way up you are flying. This time I was convinced that we were flying straight and level and not taking any evasive action, and knowing how heavily defended the coast was I urged Dick to 'Throw it about a bit' (later he told me never to do that again as he nearly turned us upside-down in consequence). Suddenly I saw blue sky above so told Dick to dive and before long I could see the ground below so told him to climb. In no time at all we emerged at 1,500 feet into brilliant sunshine, and there was not a cloud to be seen ahead.

There developed a furious row over the intercom between Dick and myself as to whether or not we should go on. I was all for 'living to fight another day', and the argument terminated abruptly with a stream of light flak which came soaring up towards us. Round we turned for home and I yelled to Dick to open the bomb doors as I had no intention of taking our bombs back with us if I could see anything worth dropping them on. I looked as hard as I could but there was nothing but flat fields below. As we crossed the coast we saw a sunken ship just off the beach and nearly bombed it but decided that it was hardly worthwhile – it was just as well that we did not do so and claim a ship sunk because when we returned Intelligence informed us that it had been sunk in 1916! In all this time we had not seen another Boston nor did we all the way home, and the time was spent wondering whether the others had gone on and we were the only ones who had turned back. In the circuit at Swanton Morley I anxiously looked on the ground for signs of any other returned aircraft but could see nothing. We were very relieved when we landed and found that all the others were in fact already back. This turned out to be the last low-level operation attempted by Bostons on the squadron and illustrated the fact that the decision to turn back when conditions were not favourable was often the hardest to make. It was not a case of being brave but of feeling ashamed of what your friends would think if you did not 'press on regardless'. This attitude lost many good crews.

That night I was moved over to the officers' mess. We were now living on the station and as the accommodation in the mess itself was limited most junior officers had to sleep in a nearby airmen's barrack block which had been converted for our use. As I stored my kit a very charming pilot who had been an Army officer and who was rather older than the rest of us came over, held out his hand and said 'Congratulations, welcome to the officers' mess'. This was in sharp contrast to the rather ribald attitude of the rest of my friends but I remember it gave me a glow of satisfaction; it had been a long and at times weary road. I was to see this pilot crash into the Channel in flames alongside us four weeks later.

That night I was fitted out in a Canadian observer's best uniform complete with cap and overcoat and taken into the local village of Dereham, where they told me mysteriously that I could join the 'Club'. This turned out to be the refreshment room on the local railway station where, miracle of miracles, there seemed to be an unending supply of bottled Bass. Sad to relate the evening had the usual and inevitable ending and after the ceremonial 'wetting' of my commission it was a very bedraggled pilot officer who fell into bed that night. The luxury of a batman was rather marred in the morning as the expression on his face clearly said 'Another drunken so-and-so to look after'.

On 23 December we took off in Boston Z2261 on a Circus operation against the docks at St Malo. Because of the distance from Norfolk to St Malo we had to land at Exeter to refuel. Exeter was the station from which some of our fighter escort were provided and after refuelling we were very annoyed to find that we had been given a full half-hour to take off and get into formation before the fighter boys came up to join us. We considered this an insult and took off in pairs on the runway just as the fighters did, two just getting airborne, two half-way down the runway, and two just beginning to roll. The result of this was that we spent some twenty-five minutes going round and round Exeter in tight formation at ground level. The town had been badly bombed and everybody came out into the streets to stare up at the twelve Bostons in tight formation going round and round. Just for good measure, when the fighters had joined us we made a last run over the roofs of Exeter, twelve Bostons and some hundred and twenty Spitfires. The traffic came to a complete halt below and no wonder, as the noise alone must have been quite something. Then followed the long low-level flight across the Channel, the Spitfires looking both beautiful and reassuring as they dipped and rose alongside us, and the first sight of a lonely lighthouse, which the whole air armada swept past although the occupants were no doubt giving the news of our coming to the enemy. Up went the noses, the engines increased their deep roar and the climb to 10,000 feet had begun.

The docks at St Malo appeared below and the run-in began, the fighters pulling discreetly away from us to the landward as the flak came up and burst among us with the usual German accuracy. The formation weaved and dived, weaved and climbed until the actual bombing run when all steadied out and the flak got closer and closer. The most trying moment came when the observer in the leading Boston went on the air and gave the order 'Bomb doors open' as there followed the bombing run, during which all aircraft had to fly straight and level which, of course, enabled the flak to become extremely accurate. Corrections to the bombing run could be heard over the air as 'Left, left, steady', or 'Right – steady' and finally 'Bombing, bombing, bombs gone', upon which all the other observers in the formation pressed their bomb buttons. In the event of a radio failure you pressed your bomb button when you saw the bombs leaving the belly of the leading aircraft. The leading observer was pretty unpopular if his bombing run lasted much more than fifteen seconds! You could feel the aircraft lift as the bombs fell away and looking down could see them falling, slightly behind but still pointing horizontally until they got nearer to the ground when it appeared that they shot forward (this was an optical illusion owing to the fact that for the first time you were seeing the bombs in relation to the ground below them and could judge their forward speed), then they disappeared from view and the next thing I saw was the white puffs of the explosions in the water of the docks. We had overshot the target. By this time we were diving steeply to the left, back in the direction of home, and our Spitfire escort was diving after us to take up the defensive screen again. If we had dived too steeply the fighter boys would have had difficulty catching us up as they had to keep weaving to protect their rear. The rest of the flight back to Exeter passed off without incident and I sat back in my little 'office' in the nose admiring the Spitfires that flew so gracefully on all sides of us. We had completed our first Circus operation. Some time later I read a poem in a paper lamenting the news that we had bombed St Malo and recalling pleasant holiday memories of the port, but to us it was a much more impersonal matter.

A little New Zealand observer and I were given forty-eight hours to get our uniforms and we left together to travel to London. At Ipswich we had to change trains, and clad in officers' raincoats and side caps which we had borrowed we went into the railway transport officer's office to be met by a very obsequious flight sergeant who escorted us to our train with a torch, much to the delight of two very recently ex-sergeants! I went on home and subsequently purchased a shockingly badly fitting best uniform. As usual after a leave I caught a train from Liverpool Lime Street station. A porter came fussing up and carried my bag. The train was full, with even the corridors crammed, but nothing daunted my porter dived inside a first-class carriage with my bag and beckoned me to follow. Lo and behold, he had found me a compartment with only one other occupant who was sitting in a corner reading a paper. This is the life, I think to myself – what a difference it makes to be an officer instead of a lowly airman. My chest swelled and the buttons strained. The train started; nobody else got into our compartment; I relaxed. Looking around me idly I could only see the shoulder-tabs of my fellow traveller who was wearing a dark blue overcoat. These shoulder tabs puzzled me, as there were no pips or crowns, which were the only things that I could recognise. Some foreigner, I thought casually, when suddenly the paper was put down and my companion got up and took his overcoat off. The sight that met my startled eye was gold braid up to the elbows and medal ribbons, row upon row, which the owner had had so long that they had barnacles on them. From being a lordly pilot officer sprawled out in the corner of the compartment I suddenly found myself very small fry sitting bolt upright on the edge of my seat. I had been put in the reserved compartment of the C-in-C Western Approaches by that fool of a porter, and it soon became evident that his staff were in the adjoining compartments, which were not altogether soundproof. I remember smirking to myself after hearing a remark about the 'Old Man' when I became conscious of a pair of very steely eyes fixed upon me. Not a word was spoken in our compartment on the whole of the journey to London; it was the most uncomfortable journey I ever spent, but at least it had the effect of showing me that I had not yet reached the top of the ladder.

The month closed with only one minor incident. On a local formation practice flight I lost my bottom hatch. I had been standing on it to adjust my bomb-sight a few seconds before it blew off and sat there with my feet dangling over a large hole. I had always wanted to make a parachute jump and for some time contemplated taking my parachute out of its stowage, clipping it on and slipping out but was deterred by the fact that I would probably have been chopped up by the propellers of one of the aircraft behind us in the formation. I had a friend in navigation school who was keen to jump and I heard later that he did so on some pretext or other while his aircraft, a Blenheim, was flying close to the coast. He misjudged the wind, however, was blown out to sea and drowned, which confirmed everyone's view that he was a pretty poor navigator anyway!

I notice from my log that both my flight commander and CO had gone on rest by the month end and that Squadron Leader Porter was now flight commander and Wing Commander Warfield the CO. I recently read a book in which I learned that my first CO was made a group captain and was subsequently killed flying to Norway.

CHAPTER 5

Ferrying Bostons to North Africa, 1943

On 21 January 1943 we took off in Boston AL702 on a Circus operation against the docks at Cherbourg but did not bomb because cloud obscured the target. The orders about bombing in the occupied countries were very strict, and under no circumstances were we allowed to drop bombs at random. A very nice cheery pilot who was on our course at OTU but who had been posted to another squadron brought back a film after a low-level attack on an aerodrome in France which showed clearly that one of his bombs had 'bounced' off the aerodrome and hit a house. The last film showed an old lady running down the steps with the collapsing house hanging poised above her. He was taken off operations and we never heard of him again.

On 29 January we took off in Boston AL269 to attack the large railway viaduct at Morlaix in France on another Circus operation. This large viaduct carried a lot of military rail traffic to southern France. As we were still regarded as a new crew we were flying in the left-hand position of the last vic of three, in other words, tailend charlie. The outward trip passed without incident and as we approached the viaduct at our usual height of 10,000 feet I noticed that at either end of the viaduct were some very pretty little houses. Being very keen in those days I pressed my bomb button a fraction of a second before the leader and watched the bombs closely all the way down until the first puffs of the explosions appeared, but they were not white as they had been in the dock water of St Malo, they were a horrible browny colour and they started right in the middle of the pretty little houses, crossed over the viaduct and finished right in the middle of the nice little houses on the other side. It was a long time before I got over where my bombs had landed.

The Germans had, for once, misjudged our intentions and thinking that we were about to attack the nearby aerodrome had put up a box barrage over it so we did not have much flak to worry about. Some of our fighters were caught in the box barrage as they pulled away from us on the bombing run, and this caused us some glee. As the viaduct was a short distance inland we skirted the town and headed back to the coast, maintaining our height of 10,000 feet. At the coast I saw a Boston which had been hit over the target and which was limping home all on its own. I had just told my crew how sorry I felt for the lone aircraft when our Spitfire escort started peeling off and turning back over France until we were left diving towards the sea without a Spitfire in sight. I felt completely naked. Suddenly our new WOp/AG called out over the intercom that there was a huge dogfight going on astern and our Spitfire must have turned back to help keep the enemy away from us. All went well for about five minutes and I was just beginning to relax when I heard our gunner yell 'Bandits, bandits, weave, weave', and this was followed by a tinny rattling sound which I realised was his twin .303 Browning machine guns firing. The formation suddenly went mad and I watched fascinated a display of aerobatic flying in tight formation the like of which I have never seen since. Our gunner would yell 'Climb, climb' and as we rose the formation would start to dive so Dick was forced to put the stick hard forward. I was alternately pressed down in my seat and then flung up against the roof of my compartment, my navigational equipment flew around everywhere, even the dust from the floor rose in clouds and still we stayed in tight formation. How we avoided touching the Boston alongside us was a miracle. The guns in the rear kept up an incessant chatter and ahead of me angry red flashes showed where the self-exploding cannon-shells of the

German fighter on our tail burst. As we flew through the bursting cannon-shells my compartment became filled with the smell of cordite and for once I felt grateful for the solid armour plating at my back. After what seemed an age I noticed that the other tailend charlie on my right, flown by the kindly ex-Army officer who had welcomed me to the officers' mess, was dropping out of the formation as the strain of this hectic bit of aerobatics became too much for him. The inevitable happened: the enemy fighters concentrated on him and soon his starboard engine was a mass of flame. I watched fascinated but helpless. Suddenly he turned towards us in a pathetic attempt to regain the formation and benefit from the protection of our combined firepower. A wing touched the sea, there was a large splash and they had gone forever. Shortly afterwards the fighters broke away (I learned later that they were the new FW190s and were stationed in the Channel Islands, which accounted for their avoiding our fighter screen).

We landed back at Exeter to refuel and on looking round the aircraft for damage found that our tail was riddled with bullet-holes. On closer inspection we discovered that these holes had been made by our own gunner firing merrily away at a Jerry who had been on our blind spot just behind and below the tail. Dick's only comment was a laconic 'Jeez, I sure would hate like hell for us to be shot down by our own gunner'. The station engineering officer inspected the damage and pronounced both main spars on the tailplane broken, and on enquiry said that he had no repair facilities and therefore our Boston would have to be dismantled and returned to a maintenance unit by road. We felt that this would be a most undignified proceeding so flew it back to base without further trouble. In passing I would mention an incident that occurred in the operations room at Exeter on our return there which illustrates what an objectionable young man I must have been in those days. The leader of the high fighter cover was being asked if he had anything to report and he replied in a lazy drawl, 'Not a thing, old boy'. This was too much for me. I glared at him and yelled across the room, 'If you had been with us you b——— well would'. I have since had good cause to feel thoroughly ashamed of that outburst as, when I had more experience of them, I realised that the fighter boys took a very dim view of themselves if they allowed the enemy to get anywhere near us.

Round about this time we had a party in the officers' mess and that month *Tee Emm** had produced an article commenting on how strange it was that junior pilot officers always liked to try on the group captain's hat at mess parties. I was in the washroom with two other pilot officers, friends of mine, when this was mentioned so without further ado they each tried on the great man's hat, complete with the 'scrambled egg' on the brim. After they had both admired themselves in the mirror it was my turn, and no sooner had I put the hat on than I realised my friends had vanished. The reason became clear when I saw that none other than the group captain himself had just walked in! Without a muscle on his face moving he calmly walked over to the wash-basin and started washing his hands. Needless to say his hat was back on its hook and I was out of there in a flash.

Air Ministry decreed that all aircrew would attend PT before breakfast. The news nearly caused a riot and in the end the wing commander himself had to go round getting officers out of bed. The squadron leaders were the hardest to get up. They made us run around the perimeter track in vest and pants, much to the glee of the groundcrews. Most of us found just walking was as much as we could do and eventually the whole scheme was dropped.

On 30 January we took off in Boston AL702 on a low-level with a difference. On reporting to the operations room we had seen the red tape marking our course. It stretched across the North Sea, crossed Holland and finished up in Germany! We all took it as a

---

* The accident casualty rate in the RAF during the war was pretty high and to combat this the Air Ministry had brought out an excellent magazine called *Tee Emm*, written in a very humorous vein but nevertheless full of sound advice.

bad joke, but unfortunately it wasn't. Mosquitos were bombing Berlin to put the great Air Marshal Göring off the air, and we were one of the many diversions laid on to give the Mosquitos a better chance of making it. It was the strangest briefing I ever had; there was no target in particular, all we were told was that once we were sure we had crossed the German frontier we were at liberty to bomb and machine-gun anything we fancied. This was a far cry from the briefings we were used to for the occupied countries. If the weather was unsuitable we had to patrol along the Dutch coast to bring out the enemy fighters. While I was drawing in the tracks on my map Dick came over to me very white-faced and whispered in my ear that he had overheard the station commander telling the chief Intelligence officer that we might get there but we would certainly never make it back home! This was not the most cheerful of news to hear before an operation but as I have said before navigators have a lot to do, which does not leave much time for worrying.

At this point I would like to digress a little. We had been having a lot of trouble with out new WOp/AG. He had a severe attack of 'twitch' and it was beginning to get us down a bit. Several times after we had all climbed aboard our aircraft and I had laid out all my navigational gear he would report some part or another of his equipment unserviceable. This meant that we would have to gather everything up and dash over to the reserve aircraft and take off in that. He was for ever reporting to Dick that smoke was coming from one or other of the engines and Dick would give him a calm, 'Yeah, yeah, I see it'. Once Dick said to me ruefully, 'One of these days that b—— is going to tell me an engine has dropped out and I will say "Yeah, Yeah", when perhaps it has'. It may be a small sidelight on the strong crew spirit that prevailed in the RAF that we never dreamed of taking our problem to higher authority. This trip proved no different. I had no sooner got my things nicely laid out than Len reported his guns unserviceable, so out we scrambled and over to the reserve aircraft; by this time the rest of the squadron were starting engines. No sooner had I sorted myself out again than lo and behold, we were told that the *wireless* was un-serviceable! By this time our own groundcrew were frantically signalling thumbs up to show that our own Boston was OK, so out again and a quick dash back with navigation bag, helmet, dinghy, parachute and all. The squadron had by now taxied to the end of the field ready for take-off but our blood was well and truly up so in we climbed, hot, dirty and in a mess. Before I could even unfold a map Dick had started up and after a very hurried cockpit check taxied at great speed to the end of the field just as the rest of the squadron flew low overhead in tight formation as was their custom. We took off with a great bellowing of engines and hurriedly set course after the fast-disappearing squadron, catching them up just after they crossed the Norfolk coast and headed out over the waves of the North Sea. The long sea crossing gave me a chance to sort myself out and apart from the oft-repeated question from Len at the back, 'How far to the enemy coast?' to which I invariably gave the answer plus twenty minutes, we were fairly well settled.

When the Dutch coast came in sight we were very relieved to see that the leader had decided the weather was not suitable: it was raining hard, and we proceeded on the alternative plan to patrol along the coast, all eyes anxiously scanning the sky. Len gave us one bad turn when he ordered 'Weave, weave', and I heard the tinny rattle of his guns over the intercom, then a small voice said 'Sorry, it was only a bit of dirt on the Perspex'. As I have said it was raining and the roof of my tiny compartment leaked badly. Wherever I put my nice new service hat it seemed to get wet, so as the spot just over my head was the only dry space I placed it carefully on my head over my flying helmet and thought no more about it. The patrol was uneventful and we all returned to base where I found that the whole squadron had been most intrigued to see me sitting in solitary state in the nose with my best hat perched on top of my flying helmet. It took some living down.

These were some of the happiest days I had on a squadron. As a very new pilot officer I was finding life in the officers' mess very pleasant. The mess at Swanton Morley had been built before the war. The ante-room was a very pleasant place with large picture windows looking out on to well-cut lawns, and roses climbed up the windows in the summer making a very pretty sight. The dining-room was just opposite the ante-room and on either side of the small main entrance corridors led away to the rooms of the senior officers. The trays of tomato and orange juice brought in before dinner by the mess waiters gave a nice touch of luxury to an ex-airman, and the sight of the station commander and the other senior officers letting their hair down at an evening party was still a novel and interesting sight to one who had had very little contact with officers over the previous three years. In short and to sound very 'snobby', I was thoroughly enjoying being an officer. Dick had been a big help in easing my path and had explained the routine of 'signing chits' for drinks, mess bills and so on.

On 2 February in Boston AL702 we took off on a sea search for George Littell and his crew. This was one of those profoundly depressing accidents which occurred from time to time on a squadron and caused a far greater drop in morale than operational losses ever did. George's was our most experienced crew and they had finished their tour of operations and were awaiting posting 'On rest'. They had taken a Boston up on an early morning flight to test the guns just out to sea. Radar had plotted them flying out about fives miles from Yarmouth when they had gradually lost height until the plot disappeared. We never found so much as an oil slick on the water.

I remember one afternoon standing by the control tower at Swanton Morley with the crew of a Lancaster that had force-landed there the night before. We were watching the squadron taking off in formation and the Lancaster pilot had just turned to me and said how he wished the rest of his pals could see the sight, when the tailend aircraft nearest to us started to bank. Over and further over it went until we were looking at the whole upper surface of it banked at 90° to the normal, with the port wing only a few feet from the ground. Everyone held their breath until ever so slowly the pilot recovered and reduced the incredible flying attitude to a steep climbing turn. The rest of the squadron had by now disappeared and we all watched this solitary aircraft banking round apparently in an attempt to land back on the aerodrome. For a while we thought that he was going to make it, but the nose dropped and the engine noise built up from a bellow to a frenzied screaming and he disappeared just over the roof of Station Headquarters. We all waited, willing him to appear again, but no – there was a horrible whooshing sound and a column of pure flame shot some 200 feet into the sky. It was suddenly very quiet, then we were all running like mad past headquarters and out of the main gate. The hedge opposite the main gate had disappeared and there was a deep furrow running across the field. Here and there, as we ran, we came across bits and pieces, all of which were burning fiercely, and I remember wondering stupidly how a machine-gun barrel could burn. When we arrived at what was left of the Boston the fire tender had already reached it and was smothering everything in foam, but even then I had a quick glimpse of what looked like a large piece of raw meat under the fuselage. It was a crew that had been at OTU with us. They were the most conscientious crew we had and the pilot, Steve Roche, and the observer, 'Tiny' Fretwell, used to call off a cockpit check to each other before every take-off. I particularly remembered Steve for his habit of stripping to the waist at the wash-basins when we were training and how white his skin had been. That thing I had seen under the fuselage: had that been all that was left of Steve or was it Tiny, the biggest navigator on the course?

It was the practice in such cases to send a pilot to the pilot's funeral and an observer to the observer's, and I was detailed to represent the squadron for the funeral of poor Tiny Fretwell. Before I left the adjutant briefed me to say as little as possible about what had happened: 'You will be able to blind them with science', he said. The first member of the family I met wore the uniform of a warrant officer in the RAF! It was a small terraced house at which I arrived in a depressing Midland town. Everyone was very kind to me in a rather dazed sort of way, but when his father explained to me that they had had some difficulty getting the coffin into the front room – 'He was such a big lad, you know' – I felt slightly sick and visions of that hunk of raw meat flashed before me, and not for the last time. The only other thing I remember was the church service. It was a cremation, and I had never attended one before. Two things broke the silence of that little place when the time arrived for the coffin to disappear: one was a most horrible squeaking from the mechanism of the conveyor belt and the other was his mother sobbing. I had never heard such sobbing before; it was the sound of a soul in torment. Those sounds remained vividly with me for many a long day afterwards. The family were more than glad to be rid of me afterwards so that they could grieve in private, so I was left in a strange city for the rest of the evening. There was only one thing to do and I did it. I got good and drunk. It did not blot out the memory but it did make it easier to bear, and I hope that if any of the good citizens saw me they did not think too unkindly of one very drunk, junior pilot officer observer.

On returning to the squadron we were sent off on seven days' leave. As operational aircrew we received very good leave compared with other members of the Services, but as time went by these frequent leaves became more and more of a strain. On the first leave after my being commissioned Dick bet me I would not change out of uniform as soon as I got home as I had done on the previous leave (which he had spent with us) but I found that I did so, mainly because I never really liked going about returning salutes and never really knew what to do if I was ignored instead of saluted. On leave one entered a world in which one was a stranger. The talk was all of the bombing, the rationing and the general war strategy, while one constantly wondered what was going on at the squadron. None of my friends were ever at home at the same time as myself, I knew no girls and the highlight of my day would be when my uncle took me to the local at lunchtime where he would proudly introduce me to what seemed, to my young eyes, a lot of very old men who would slap me on the back and pour far too much draught Bass down my gullet so that I had a job to eat the large meal that my mother had prepared with such loving care. I would never let my mother see me off at the station (the young can be very cruel), though once I caught sight of her in the crowd. As the train pulled out of Liverpool Lime Street station you could not help wondering: would you ever see this place again?

On 11 February 1943 we were on the Battle Order for a Circus operation against a ship in Boulogne harbour, but our WOp/AG had not returned from leave. He rang Dick to say he was not coming back; I heard that his wife was expecting a baby and was giving him a difficult time. Despite Dick's pleading he went LMF (Lack of Moral Fibre) and we never saw him again, so we went to Boulogne with a replacement, Flight Sergeant Bishop, a much more stoical type. We did not bomb owing to cloud over the target, so got shot at for nothing. We had landed at Ford the day before to refuel and take off at first light the next morning. Very rashly our flight commander allowed us to go out for the night and we had a riotous time in the nearby town. At about 0100 hours we all gathered in the centre of the town and endeavoured to get some taxi drivers to take us back to Ford, but they refused, saying it was outside their permitted limits. We convinced them that we were all night fighter pilots and would not be able to guarantee the safety of the area from attack if we were not taken back to Ford immediately. We made the trip in record time with a set of fearful taxi drivers who kept anxiously scanning the night sky! Later that morning I was sitting in the nose of Boston AL705 on the ground, feeling like death, with the oxygen switched on to 20,000 feet! It was the only time I went on an operation with such a hangover and the experience made me feel so ghastly that I never did it again.

On 13 February we had another go at the ship in Boulogne harbour. This time it was ringed with small anti-aircraft ships and we did bomb, the result being the complete destruction of one anti-aircraft vessel which collected the full weight of our bomb-load all to itself. On 15 February we were on another Circus operation against the same ship, which had now been moved to Dunkirk. This did not please us as the defences at Dunkirk were stronger than those at Boulogne, but again we did not bomb because of cloud obscuring the target. Once more we were on the receiving end for nothing. It was only recently, while reading an account of German commerce raiders of the war that I realised that the ship they had sent us out after was one which had sunk many of our merchant ships and was running the gauntlet back to Germany. I often wonder why we were not told of these things. I don't say we could have done any better, but it would at least have made the war a bit more personal for us.

When the squadron was taking off for an operation it was customary for all personnel who could to congregate round the flying control tower to watch. The station commander would be up on the top balcony of the tower and in all it would amount to quite a crowd. One day, as we were not on the Battle Order, we were watching when it became evident that one aircraft had retracted its undercarriage too soon. (As I have mentioned, we always made a point of whipping up the undercarriage as soon as possible.) The plane sank gradually lower and lower until the tips of the propellers started to churn into the ground, flinging up great chunks of turf. Finally the pilot switched off his engines and skidded along the grass on his belly. We all held our breath and before the plane came to halt the observer's top hatch was flung open and he leaped out and ran like a hare. Luckily the Boston did not catch fire or the bombs go off. The observer was a lanky Canadian and later in the mess we pulled his leg about the speed with which he had left the plane, to which he replied: 'Boy, I was just cruising. When I looked back, if she had been on fire I would have really got going.'

March 1943 was a happy month. On the 1st the squadron took off for Hurn on the south coast to take part in Exercise Spartan. This was a large-scale exercise as a preliminary to D-Day in which the Army and Air Force were practising close co-operation and in which a mock battle was being fought between the forces of the North and the South. The feeling of still being on a squadron but relieved, if only temporarily, from the threat of imminent death, gave us all a party feeling. We were supposed to be a mobile close support strike force and all our equipment was placed in about sixty vehicles which included a mobile kitchen. We were housed in tents and as an officer I was issued with a camp bed, a canvas bucket, a canvas wash-basin and a revolver. The permanent quarters of the aerodrome were off limits to us and for the first few days we had a very rough time getting used to tent life. I remember asking one grizzled 'Chiefy' of the ground staff how he was getting on and received an unprintable reply, as he had just broken his false teeth on an 'Issue' biscuit. Attached to our squadron was a very dashing Army captain. He arrived full of enthusiasm with a magnificent map case and set of coloured crayons which he used to draw in the front line and the opposing armies' dispositions. He had a field telephone outside his tent and he proudly informed us that he would give us the latest situation reports each morning. The first day the front line stayed static – and it remained that way for the rest of the exercise. Somewhere in the higher command the existence of our Army liaison officer had been forgotten. We were given one target to attack: it was a straight road about two miles long and reported to be packed with enemy transport. Twelve Bostons roared down the road at telegraph pole height. The only occupant was a lone civilian motor cyclist who was so shocked he ran into a ditch.

On 6 March we moved to Lasham and our ground transport followed on. All arrived safely apart from two vehicles – one contained our tents and the other the mobile kitchen, so we spent the night out in the open, cold and hungry! By now we had learned the art of camping the hard way and at night, in defiance of the blackout, fires could be seen burning merrily away in front of each tent while the occupants squatted round cooking their own succulent dishes. About this time the group captain commanding our home base at Swanton Morley flew down to see how we were getting on and brought the catering officer with him. On enquiring what we would like most when we returned to base he was given an overwhelming request for a good meal, and when on 11 March the exercise finished and we returned to Swanton Morley we had the largest steaks I have ever seen topped with fried eggs.

At the end of the month Dick and I managed to wangle a trip to the Boston maintenance unit at Hooton Park. We stayed the night at home and took off the next afternoon, which was a Sunday, in Boston BZ293. The temptation to 'beat up' my home proved too great and we did a real low-level pass over my house which took us over most of the chimney-tops in Birkenhead and caused quite a lot of consternation to the good citizens as I heard later from my parents. On the second time round we were amused to see that the entire balloon barrage of Merseyside was being wound up as rapidly as possible, as clearly they did not appreciate such a noisy disturbance on a quiet Sunday afternoon. So we took the hint and left. Irresponsible, reckless? Yes, but then we were very proud of ourselves in those days and very young and very full of the joy of life, and nobody who has not experienced it can appreciate the thrill of taking part in a real low-level 'beat-up', providing of course that you know what you are doing – and we prided ourselves on being experts. I remember that once the Aerodrome Defence were foolish enough to request a mock attack by our squadron to give them some practice. It was hurriedly cut short after a series of the most hair-raising exhibitions of low-level flying I have ever seen. Bostons were roaring past cutting the turf with the tips of their propellors and tearing in between buildings in a vertical position with the tip of one wing only a matter of feet from the ground. Ground staff were scattering in all directions very much like the sheep and cattle in our low-flying areas.

On 13 April 1943 we were detached to our satellite aerodrome, West Raynham, for ferry duties. We had lost our Bostons and were to re-equip on Mitchell aircraft, but first of all some of us had to fly our Bostons out to the Middle East. Before going to West Raynham we were all injected against yellow fever with a special serum flown up from London, and given a little certificate without which we were assured we would not be allowed to set foot in North Africa. Needless to say nobody ever asked us for it. More about those injections later! At West Raynham we saw old Z2261, now resplendent in tropical camouflage with tropical air filters and long-range tanks fitted in the bomb bay; there were also many messages scrawled inside, such as 'Remember me your fitter, Betty Smith'! This was the aircraft we had been detailed to deliver. We did a full fuel load air test at 6,000 feet and on 14 April flew down to Portreath in Cornwall, which was our first staging post. One crew, the pilot of which was a nineteen-year-old Canadian who was forever getting into trouble, arrived some hours after us with a hair-raising tale. They had mistaken an aerodrome some ten miles north for Portreath and had landed there. The runway was, however, too short for a Boston and they had come to a halt only a matter of yards from a sheer cliff which dropped straight down to the sea below.

Adverse weather conditions gave us a four-day break at Portreath, which gave us an opportunity to explore the delightful Cornish countryside, and I remember how impressed we were with the efficiency of the local bus service. Our briefing was that we were to fly singly to Gibraltar and there hand over our aircraft to other pilots who would fly them on to North Africa. We would return as passengers the next day in an aircraft provided by Transport Command. We were each given an impressive document to the effect that once our ferry duties were over we were to be given every facility to return to the United Kingdom. At 0730 hours on 18 April we took off in a very heavily laden Boston Z2261, to begin what was to turn out to be a most incredible adventure.

We had been given the choice of crossing the Bay of Biscay at either sea level or 10,000 feet; we chose the latter to avoid the Ju88s which prowled this area. Owing to the quantity of spares we carried it was not possible to open the bottom hatch in the gunner's compartment, so we were completely blind underneath, but we decided that this was a risk worth taking. In the nose I had so much gear stowed that it was impossible for me even to move my feet. We left the glorious deep blue water surrounding Cornwall and headed south climbing steadily. My chief concern on the trip was to give Dick the times for changing over from the various auxiliary tanks we carried. Half-way across the Bay we were droning along steadily at 10,000 feet; there was not a cloud in the sky and the sun shone warmly upon us. I called up Dick and told him that it was time to change over some of the auxiliary tanks. There was no reply. After several more calls, each a little louder than the last, Dick replied: he had been fast asleep! Eventually Cape Finisterre hove in sight and we began to fly round the coast of Spain. Although it would have been much quicker to fly over Spain we had been briefed not to do so, as any aircraft having to make a forced landing on Spanish territory had their crews thrown into civil gaols for bringing guns into the country illegally, and as this was a civil offence the British consul was powerless to help. We had heard that Spanish gaols were not pleasant places. I have never been to Spain, but the coastline from Cape Finisterre to Gibraltar certainly looked bleak and grim to me. After six hours' uneventful flying in solitary confinement in the nose the famous Rock of Gibraltar came in sight, and when I saw the tiny ribbon of a runway that we were to land on projecting out into the sea at both ends I nearly died of fright! Thanks to Dick's skill and the Boston's excellent brakes (without which it was reckoned she would roll for five miles after landing) we got down safely and taxied off the runway.

At that time Gibraltar had so many aircraft that parking was a very difficult problem; there were all types imaginable parked nose to tail, Beaufighters, Beauforts, Blenheims, Bisleys, Albemarles, Marylands, and more, and huge notices proclaimed the fact that on no account were engines to be opened up in the parking area to prevent damage to other aircraft. On dropping my hatch I found that my legs were so cramped that I could not stand on them for some time but the sight of the white clouds streaming off the top of the rock in the sunshine like the smoke from a ship's funnel dispelled all sense of personal discomfort. Gradually the remainder of the squadron arrived, the big tails of the Bostons sticking way up above the surrounding aircraft, and now their desert camouflage no longer looked strange. We all reported to the operations room confident that our task was done, only to be told that we would be briefed the next morning for the flight to North Africa! When we protested that our orders had been to bring the Bostons to Gibraltar they pointed out, not unreasonably, that there was hardly room at Gib. for aircraft to be left lying about so, not having seen North Africa, we agreed to have a go.

That night, I regret to say, was not spent touring the ancient Rock but instead was spent in the officers' mess having a party. The sergeants did the same in the sergeants' mess and our Canadian friend Sergeant S. hardly endeared himself to the local inhabitants by insisting on taking a shower at about midnight fully clothed. His crew's endeavours to remove him resulted in the pipes in the showers being pulled down.

Our briefing the next morning was to fly to Biskra in North Africa. We were told to fly in formations of three on account of enemy aircraft and given a complicated set of instructions regarding the signals we had to send informing Biskra of our intended time of arrival. I was issued with a chart of the area and shocked the navigation officer when I told him that I required a map, not a chart. After a frantic search the best they could produce was a map of North Africa to a scale of 1 in 2 million which was little better than a school atlas – but it had to do.

We led the first formation of three aircraft and in our usual showy manner took off in formation. This had not been seen on the Rock before, and I believe we gave them a nasty few minutes when No. 2 disappeared from sight below the level of the runway after take-off and skimmed the sea through being caught in the turbulence of our slipstream. It also shook No. 2, who happened to be Sergeant S. Taking off from the Rock at the same time as us was a veritable armada of other aircraft, all with the same destination. They were chiefly Beaufighters, Beauforts and Bisleys, in all some two hundred aircraft. We flew fairly high and when I saw an aircraft carrier ahead with an attending escort of destroyers I swung the formation round to give it a wide berth, knowing all too well the Navy's understandable trigger-happy attitude, and was amazed to see the Beaufighters, which were at sea level, carry on and fly right over the flight deck of the carrier! The Navy's reaction was a picture, and as we left they were scrambling fighters as fast as they could. The North African coast was covered in cloud and as the mountain ranges went up to 3,000 feet or so we climbed up above the cloud. All the time, Frank, our wireless operator, was sending out messages giving our estimated time of arrival at Biskra and as instructed I amended our arrival time every half-hour. After three and a half hours' flying Biskra came in sight and we joined the circuit which rapidly filled up as Beaufighters, Beauforts, etc., joined us. On landing we taxied up to a tent, which was the only sign of habitation in that barren area, and I jumped out of my bottom hatch as Dick switched off the engines.

Outside the tent stood a flight lieutenant in very sun-bleached khaki staring in bewilderment, open-mouthed, at the two hundred or so aircraft now in the circuit. He soon made it clear to me that he had no idea any of us were coming – what happened to our wireless messages I never found out. He was all that remained of a rear party left behind when the rest of the ground staff had moved forward. We were told gloomily that we would get nothing to eat as there had been a fire in the cookhouse the day before. Eventually, when all the aircraft had landed, with the exception of a Polish wing commander leading the Beaufighters, who had crashed into the mountains, transport was found to take us into Constantine for the night while our aircraft were refuelled by a scratch groundcrew.

The Germans had only recently left Constantine and it was in a bit of a mess. We were put up in an hotel and all I can remember is that apart from the drains being blocked the lights kept going out so we sat drinking abominable-tasting red wine alternately in electric light and candlelight until we ran out of matches and we all went to bed.

The next morning we were taken out to the airfield where we discovered that one Canadian flight sergeant pilot and his English navigator were missing. They were an ill-assorted pair: the pilot was a great hulk of a man with arms like a gorilla and his navigator was an English 'Right Honourable' and acted the part. As we stood in a group at the entrance to the airfield gazing anxiously down the road leading to town we saw a little cloud of dust approaching slowly. When it got nearer we could make out the figure of the Canadian pilot with his navigator slung over his back like a sack of coals. When he reached us the sight was even more incredible – both were unshaven, the flight sergeant had one single stripe left hanging down from his sleeve, his pockets were stuffed with French francs and his navigator was out cold while he was very merry indeed. Apparently they had spent the night in the Arab quarter playing cards; how they had avoided getting their throats cut I don't know. None of us were looking very smart by this time as we were all in our blue uniforms and had only the clothes we stood up in. Dick had a big oil stain across the shoulders of his tunic obtained while looking at the engines which, like the rest of the aircraft, had had no attention whatever from the groundcrews since leaving England.

We all filed into the tent to be given the briefing for the next stage of our journey – to Cairo! When we got our breath back we asked why Cairo, and were told patiently by the sun-bleached flight lieutenant that we had to go to Cairo as this was the next stop on the journey to India! This was too much, and we retired to hold a council of war. The result of this was that we told a startled flight lieutenant: 'This far and no further.' I think that what really decided us to take this stand was the state of our aircraft which had not had, nor seemed as if they would ever have, a proper check-up. I have often wondered since what would have happened if we had gone on to Cairo without protest. Who knows, we might have spent the rest of the war flying on and on like some aerial Flying Dutchman; Dick might be alive today; we might all be dead; who knows? What happened in fact was that whereas all the other aircraft took off the Bostons remained, tails sticking up proudly in the desert, awaiting the results of a series of frantic signals.

After a lot of fuss we were talked into taking the aircraft to their correct destination which was, we were told, a nearby airfield and we took off in formation for Oulmene. The tough Canadian flight sergeant was still very merry and his navigator was still out cold so he unceremoniously bundled him into the nose of their Boston and took off. His formation flying was atrocious and he frightened the life out of us as he came in too close, then was forced to break away. This meant that as we saw the belly of his Boston sliding in towards us we knew that he could not see where we were. Eventually he gave up the attempt to keep in formation and dived away towards the mountains below, and for a while we could see him chasing up and down the valleys beneath us till he was lost to view. On arriving at Oulmene it was raining hard and once again the airfield seemed to consist of a large expanse of nothing surrounded by desert. This time the only thing in sight was a caravan which displayed no signs of life so we taxied up to it, switched off our engines and ran over in the pouring rain. Inside was a weary-looking flying officer surrounded by piles and piles of letters. He explained that he was the squadron adjutant, the unit having moved forward the day before, and he had stayed behind to censor the mail. He showed us the location of the squadron on our school-atlas type maps, and after awaiting the arrival of a considerably more sober Canadian flight sergeant we took off again and eventually located our true destination just outside Tunis, which had not yet fallen. The Right Honourable navigator had by now come to and was expressing extreme astonishment at his unfamiliar surroundings.

On reporting to the station adjutant we were welcomed with open arms and told to report to A Flight the next morning. We patiently explained that we were only ferry crews and wished to return to the UK forthwith; to prove the point we even produced our official documents which said just that. He roared with laughter and said, 'Everyone who comes here has those, how do you think we get our replacement crews?' (I have since read the memoirs of no less a person than Lord Tedder who strongly denied the allegations of Arthur Harris that his ferry crews were so treated.) This was really too much for us, brought up to believe in democracy. We took our flying kit out of our aircraft, wished the faithful old Bostons goodbye and went to our respective messes for a meal. For the first time it really came home to me that we were now a long long way from Swanton Morley. Without our trusty Bostons England was no longer a mere nine or ten hours' flying time away; it was many thousands of miles with plenty of water in between. In a very depressed mood we went to bed. Looking back it occurs to me that a tour of operations in North Africa on Bostons would have been quite pleasant. The Germans were about to surrender in Tunis and Dick may have been alive today if we had stayed, but we were fiercely loyal to our own squadron and this attempt to shanghai us strongly offended our sense of justice, so with common consent all three crews had breakfast the next morning, collected our flying kit and walked out of the main gates. There we stood at the side of a dusty road in North Africa, nine very scruffy-looking aircrew dressed in blue with parachutes, helmets, Mae Wests, flying boots and navigation bags, wondering what would happen next.

A large convoy of big American trucks came thundering down the road towards us and as they were in convoy we did not even attempt to thumb a lift, but to our surprise they pulled up in a cloud of dust in front of us and the leading driver put his head out of the cab and told us to jump aboard, one to each truck. This we did and there followed a ride I shall always remember. The huge trucks kept up an average speed of about 40 m.p.h., nose to tail. From time to time the gum-chewing American drivers would open their cab doors, stand with one foot on the running-board and the other on the accelerator and conduct a shouted conversation with their buddy in the next truck. Whenever they came across any Arabs walking at the side of the road they whooped with joy, banged the outside of their door panels with one hand and drove straight at the Arabs, who scattered for their lives. With no small feeling of relief we were eventually dropped off on the outskirts of Constantine.

In no time at all we were surrounded by the inevitable horde of small Arab children who were pressed into service as carriers. It was a very curious caravan that met the eyes of an air commodore driving past in a staff car. He instructed his driver to pull in to the side of the road, got out of his car and gave us all a lecture about the necessity of keeping up appearances when overseas. He then flicked an imaginary spot of dust off his immaculate khaki uniform, stepped into his car and drove off. We were to meet again. The little caravan trudged on its weary way until we reached Constantine and there we had a difficult time trying to pay off our small bearers. With the usual sense of British justice we attempted to give those with the heaviest loads the largest amount but their spokesman would have none of it and we had to settle for a flat rate for all. We spent the next day exploring Constantine. This was not very enjoyable as the few Service canteens were either for officers or NCOs, and we consisted of a party of two officers, Dick and me, and seven NCOs. We refused to split up and with our queer sense of unit loyalty trudged the hot and dusty streets. I personally felt very embarrassed by the revolver I was wearing as the swarms of urchins that followed us everywhere were intrigued by these weapons and did everything but take them out of their holsters. I was too worried about losing the wretched thing to do anything but wear it. Money was now becoming a serious problem as we had used up all the loose change we carried, so by common consent we broke open the escape kits with which we had been issued and started to live a little on the dollars and francs enclosed.

The day after our arrival at Constantine we heard of a nearby American Dakota unit and the next morning, appropriately enough St George's day, 23 April, we trooped out to their airfield waving, in a rather pathetic manner, our authorities for a quick return to the UK. This time, however, we had a very different reception. 'Sure', they said, 'You bring the planes out here, Bud, and we will get you back again', and at 1330 hours we took off in Dakota 118382: pilot, Top Sergeant Brown; destination, Maison Blanche just outside Algiers. We were very bucked to be on our way again and felt that all our troubles were now over; the motto became 'Fly American'. The trip, however, turned out to be one of the most terrifying I have ever made. The Dakota was strictly a utility model with hard metal seats facing each other down both sides of the fuselage, and the crew of three spent the time standing around the pilot, talking and chewing gum. We were flying above cloud and crossing the 3,000-foot range of mountains I mentioned earlier. The navigator glanced at his watch, tapped the pilot on the shoulder, down went the nose into the clouds and at about 1,000 feet, much to our relief, we broke cloud over flat ground near Algiers.

Once on the ground at Maison Blanche we made straight for the nearest American unit but alas our priority chits were to no avail. A slightly embarrassed American officer informed us that there had been a spot of difficulty lately about such flights. (We found out later that Royal Air Force personnel stationed in North Africa had been picked up by the Service police in London, having nipped home for a weekend via the American Army Air Corps.) Now all such trips had to be made via an RAF transportation officer. We duly arrived at the office of a sour-faced squadron leader who glanced at our priority chits in a half-hearted manner and then made arrangements, somewhat reluctantly, for us to go out to an aircrew transit camp on the cliffs just outside Algiers. This turned out to be a pretty little French chalet on the top of the cliffs, run by a surly flying officer pilot. The reason for his ungraciousness became apparent when we discovered that he was already drawing rations for about thirty aircrew who did not exist, so we cramped his style of living somewhat. Apparently everyone at RAF Base Headquarters then forgot about us and we spent some very pleasant days by the sea. One morning in the midst of an early morning session at the bar the morose flying officer came in and announced with evident pleasure that a call had just come through from Base Headquarters, Algiers, that we were to report there immediately. Upon asking how we were to get there he said that he had no transport but there was a radio location station further up the road with plenty so I was deputised to go and collect a truck, despite the fact that at that time I could not drive.

Up the road I went until I came to another pretty little bungalow outside which were four RAF 15-cwt trucks. On entering I was welcomed by four ground-type officers and pressed to have a drink; this I did, then another, then another. Eventually the senior officer, an ancient flight lieutenant of First World War vintage, staggered off to bed. All this time I had been aware of a series of crashes and the sounds of breaking crockery coming from the direction of the kitchen. Nobody took the slightest notice of this and all sat drinking steadily. At last I could not restrain my curiosity and asked what was happening. I was told quite casually that it was only the cook and that they were waiting for him to sober up so that they could have lunch. After a few more drinks I plucked up courage to ask if I could borrow a truck. They said of course I could and they were sure that if the CO, the ancient flight lieutenant, had been awake he would be delighted to say yes, so I departed from that Alice-in-Wonderland scene and somehow managed to drive one of the trucks back to our rest camp. The rest of the boys had not wasted their time either while I had been away and were all in a very merry mood, but it was wisely decided that someone with a little more experience would do the driving. As we passed the Radio Location bungalow all the officers inside rushed out waving to us to stop and I suddenly feared that they must have sobered up enough to have regretted their generosity, but no – it was only to ask us all to have a drink with them. When we eventually left and reached RAF Base Headquarters, apart from being a sorry sight we were in a very sorry condition. One flying officer, one pilot officer and seven senior NCOs were told very coldly that they had to see a certain air commodore. When ushered into his presence it turned out to be none other than the air commodore who had stopped us on the road to Constantine, but fortunately he did not seem to recall the incident.

Looking back on it I suppose that the poor man was too overcome by the sight we presented. It was the most fantastic interview I have ever had with a senior officer. He started off by telling us that we had been posted as deserters as they had been looking all over North Africa for us, and for this we could be shot in wartime. This dire statement had no effect whatever on the assembled throng. Dick, his hat pushed to the back of his head, was leaning on a bookcase which was doing its best to hold him up. Sergeant Bishop, with both hands deep in his trouser pockets, slowly rocked back and forth repeating over and over again, 'I have only been married a month', till at last the air commodore broke off his speech, turned to him and said, in a fatherly manner, 'There, there, I know it is hard on you, it is hard on all of us'. This seemed to terminate the interview so we all shuffled out and returned to the rest camp. Apparently signals flew between Algiers and Air Ministry, the result of which was that Air Ministry plumped for us to be returned to the UK. Not to be defeated easily RAF Base Headquarters, Algiers, sent us back by the slowest route they could think of, and we embarked on the battleship HMS *Rodney* which was returning to her home port after taking part in the North African landings.

Rodney was packed with an assortment of Fleet Air Arm pilots and other naval officers returning for various reasons to the UK, and as two junior officers we were put into the gunroom; the rest of our crew messed with the petty officers. The Navy were, as usual, the perfect hosts, although their looks clearly showed that although they had never really believed all the talk they had heard about the scruffy RAF we were proving that it was indeed true. I was very amused to notice the attitude of the various junior naval officers to each other. One said to me in all seriousness, 'That chap gets on my nerves; he will argue with me and I am two weeks his senior'. As an officer in a Service in which you had to be at least two ranks senior to anybody just to get listened to, this did appear a little strange!

In the wardroom gin and lime was 3*d* per tot and although the ship's officers drank very little while at sea, we had nothing much else to do. One day, while leaning over the rail and moodily surveying the heaving ocean, I was rudely interrupted by a breathless messenger who informed me that I was wanted by the captain of marines right away. Somewhat mystified I allowed myself to be led below along a maze of corridors. Suddenly six large marines, all in perfect step, came marching in single file towards us. As I flattened myself against the wall of the corridor to let them pass I recognised the dishevelled figure of my pilot Dick staggering after them, closely followed by another six marines. As this strange procession swept past I heard Dick say, 'I used to think that the Royal Navy was OK but now I think they are p—— poor'. I was beginning to realise why the captain of marines wanted to see me. In the captain's cabin I met what was perhaps the most chilling reception of my young life; I was told very coldly and curtly that Dick was under close arrest and I was to be his escorting officer. In addition, the rest of our crews were under close arrest in the ship's cells. Glad to get away I was taken along to a cabin which was distinguished by the fact that it had a wooden grating jammed under the door handle and another grating across the corridor so that it was impossible to open from the inside (the Navy knew a thing or two). Looking through the wooden ventilation slats into this cabin I saw that its furniture consisted of one bunk screwed into the wall and one chair which was now smashed to bits, on the remains of which Dick was sitting. He always got violent when very drunk. I was given the cabin next door and stayed there for the rest of the voyage, my meals being brought to me.

Gradually the story filtered down to me (Dick was no help as he was still very merry). The aircraft carrier HMS *Formidable*, followed by the battleships HMS *Nelson* and HMS *Rodney*, were steaming in line on their majestic way through the Bay of Biscay with a large screen of protecting destroyers. They were returning to England after having played a not inconsiderable part in the invasion of North Africa (I was told *Rodney* was only kept afloat by her pumps owing to the strain to the hull of repeated broadsides). No doubt the captain on his bridge felt that all was right with the world until there burst upon this scene of naval might one very drunk and dishevelled RAF sergeant who staggered up the deck in front of the mighty sixteen-inch guns, shouted 'Good old Navy,' and promptly fell flat on his face! What followed was as inevitable as night following day. The captain was neither amused nor pleased at the compliment. The officer of the watch was hastily despatched to investigate. A party in the petty officer's mess was discovered at which, horror of horrors, an RAF officer was present, and retribution fell swiftly. One of our gallant band who had passed out earlier had been hidden under a bunk by some kindly petty officer, but apparently the ship took a roll at the wrong moment and out rolled his inanimate body, so there were no escapees. Our air gunner had fallen off a table while making an impromptu speech and when I next saw him his head was swathed in white bandages. It seemed that the ship's petty officers had helped the party along with liberal tots from illicitly stored rum rations and this, together with the bottles of cheap red wine our boys had brought along, kept them merry for two more days!

The time came when HMS *Rodney* arrived at her home port and signals were despatched to a nearby Australian Coastal Command flying boat base requesting a launch to remove the nuisances. On deck a sorry sight met my eyes as I surveyed our party, but ironically I was the only one worried. The rest were still very merry and were treating the whole thing as a great joke. After a little persuasion they all clambered aboard the RAF launch and we landed at the flying boat base where the usual reception committee of Service police were waiting. At this stage Dick suddenly awoke to the fact that his small case containing all his worldly possessions was not about so I headed back in the launch on my own to the *Rodney*. By this time she was an even more impressive sight. She had 'manned ship', her assembled crew looking magnificent, there was a band on the forward turret and she was slowly moving into harbour. I regret to say that at the time I was so preoccupied with the missing case that all this barely registered with me so that I felt genuinely indignant when the officer of the watch, standing rigidly at attention complete with sword at his side, only gave an angry wiggle of one hand as a sign that he had heard my repeated hails to throw down the bag, and that hand clearly said 'Buzz OFF'. We made a couple of circuits of that mighty ship in our little launch and yelled and yelled but no one took any notice, and looking back on the incident I suppose we should have felt grateful that they did not open fire on us! When *Rodney* was alongside we phoned the ship but no one would admit to having ever set eyes on the bag (I expect it went down tied to the anchor!)

The group captain of the flying boat base was a very nice man and put Dick under open arrest so that he could eat in the mess that night. Nevertheless, he arranged for us to proceed back to our home base at Swanton Morley by train first thing the next morning with myself as escorting officer. The boys were still feeling very happy and I had a difficult time persuading them not to make a night of it in London. As we travelled across London in the Underground I was amazed at the consideration we received:

porters fell over themselves to carry our flying kit and the crowds all stood on one side to let us through. As we filed through a ticket barrier all became clear as one ticket collector turned to the other and said, 'Poor devils, must have been shot down last night'. Our appearance, our flying kit and our air gunner's bandages must have done the trick, which just goes to prove that there is no justice – because later when I HAD been shot down and could only stand on one leg I had to do just that from London to Liverpool in a crowded train corridor despite a first class ticket! We arrived back at Swanton Morley without further incident. The eventual punishment was three months' loss of seniority which bothered them not at all, especially as most, including Dick, were dead within the next six months.

Once again we returned to a change in commanding officers. Our new CO was Wing Commander Tait, a very charming man but afflicted with a severe case of 'twitch'. I often felt that the Royal Air Force put a very severe burden on its flight and squadron commanders, as not only did they have to carry out operational duties but when on the ground they had to cope with all the day-to-day problems of running a squadron. We used to refer to 'twitch' in a jocular manner, but in fact it was a pathetic sight as it was caused by the victim's nerves being in such a state that certain muscles, generally in the face or neck, would twitch uncontrollably. In nearly every case I knew the victim would soon be lost on operations, and I feel sure that it would have been far better to send such people on rest to recover, to avoid these deaths. One thing I learned on a squadron was that courage is a commodity that is expendable and that all men have a breaking point. This point comes sooner with some than others, but come it does eventually to all. Most of us lived in dread, not of death, but of showing our fear to others. Some became over-loud and over-talkative, others became over-quiet, and a lot of the 'high spirits' that is mentioned in reference to aircrew activities was only a method of relieving what was becoming an unbearable inner tension. There comes a point where your body seems to rebel against being continually subjected to the chance of sudden death, and at this stage you are no longer a really efficient fighting man. I feel the same fault lay in all the Services, and probably always will. Once you are classed as a fighting man with 'battle experience' you have to carry on and on. This, of course, is true but not always were you a veteran; you had to learn, and in modern warfare there are so very many behind you who will never be asked to learn. Many a good fighting man had died through lack of rest, and when he died someone else had to take his place anyway. If he had been resting in the rear he would have been a powerful reserve, as well as a man who would see that the fighting men got the support they deserved. Strange to say the ones who would resist it most would be some of the most battle weary, but it should be insisted upon as a necessity. An aircraft is not put on an operation unless it is perfectly fit, but what about the crew? Still, this is going ahead somewhat as at this time I was still full of beans and not at all 'flak-happy' as far as I can tell.

At about this time one of the other squadrons of No. 2 Group was unlucky enough to be re-equipped with American Ventura aircraft. They were very like the Lockheed Hudson in appearance, having a round tubby fuselage, and were entirely unsuited for the task to which they were put. Their only good point was the fact that, if you so desired, you could take a bicycle along with you in one when cadging a lift on leave. Their operational end was hastened when a whole squadron was lost on one operation. The wing commander, who was leading, survived as a prisoner of war and was awarded the Victoria Cross as a consolation, which he richly deserved but which did not help those who died. That night, I was told, the ground staff officers helped the lone surviving flying officer pilot, who did not take part in the raid, and who was now acting CO, to get well and truly tight.

CHAPTER 6

No. 226 Squadron – Mitchells

In May 1943 we flew for the first time in a Mitchell Mk II EL673 on circuits and landings. To us the Mitchell seemed a very large and ugly aircraft after the Boston. It lacked the Boston's trim lines and deep narrow fuselage and big tail. In fact it had twin tails and the wings had an 'anhedral' which gave them the appearance of drooping. We entered through a bottom hatch into the navigation compartment; this meant that on leaving the aircraft you had to walk to the rear to clear the propellers, whereas on the Boston you had had to walk forward to clear them. This took a bit of remembering but was well worthwhile! The Mitchell had a tricycle undercarriage like the Boston, carried a bigger bomb-load (4 × 1,000 lb) and had a power-operated upper turret with twin .5-inch machine guns. There was a co-pilot's seat, automatic pilot, and a very roomy navigation compartment from which a tunnel ran under the pilot's seat up to the bomb aimer's compartment in the nose, in which there was also a .3-inch machine gun. In all I had five seats to choose from! There was another tunnel running above the bomb bay to the roomy wireless operator's compartment at the rear which also had the upper gunner's turret in it, so now we could all get to each other at last. To do the upper turret full honours our crews were now enlarged to four and we got ourselves an air gunner, Sergeant N. by name. (The Americans fielded a crew of six in their Mitchells but then they had more 'bods' to call on.) We observers soon realised that the only place from which we could operate was the nose, but strange to relate we were now forbidden to be in there during landing or take-off, so generally sat in the co-pilot's seat at these times. To get into the nose you lay on your back, gripped two rails mounted in the roof of the tunnel and pulled yourself through into the nose. Once again the visibility was very good as you were a long way forward of the wings and even the engines. There was a comfortable seat and a smaller bicycle-type seat in the nose for use when using the bomb-sight. The wireless gear was of the usual fabulous US pattern and we even had a radio compass on which you could get the Forces Programme with amazing clarity. On the other hand, the intercommunication system had been designed for the American throat microphones and did not work at all well with our RAF-type mouth microphones so that at times it was nearly impossible to understand each other. Each intercom position had a switch with five different channels and an overriding position which could cut in on any of them. On training flights this was very necessary as you could never raise any of the crew on the normal channels; they would all be listening in on the Forces Programme on the radio compass!

In my usual pessimistic manner I had worked out my own exit from a Mitchell in case of trouble and also what I considered was the best 'ditching' position to take up. (Ditching was the RAF expression for coming down in the sea.) The navigation compartment was in front of the bomb bay and a set of steps led up forward into the pilot's compartment. The pilot's seat had the usual armour-plated back but the co-pilot's seat did not have a back; instead there was an armour-plated door which hinged back when not in use. When in position protecting the co-pilot's seat this was, I thought, an excellent place to stand, facing the rear. My theory was to be put to the test all too soon.

The remainder of May and the whole of June were taken up with intensive practice flying. The pilots found that the Mitchell was a very much more difficult aircraft to fly in formation than the Boston, but for myself I found the ability to move about was a distinct advantage.

On 19 July, the whole squadron moved up to RAF Station, Drem, just outside Edinburgh, for a Fighter Affiliation Course. At Drem was a French Spitfire squadron, whose method of attacking our formation was frightening. They would come at us head-on, then bank vertically and slice through our formation like a knife through butter. One day the Duke of —— paid us a visit. On one side of the perimeter track the aircraft were lined up – even the propellers had been lined up – and on the other side we stood in as neat ranks as could be expected from aircrew. Around the track towards us rolled three majestic cars. When the leading car stopped in front of us our wing commander stepped smartly forward, opened the rear door and stood at the salute, whereupon the door on the other side of the car opened and out stepped the Duke! This was too much for our sense of humour and a loud burst of laughter came from our ranks. The Duke gave us a startled look and decided to inspect the aircraft instead of us, so we stood there until the inspection of the aircraft was over, saying unkind things to each other about how we hoped the undercarriage of the plane he was in would collapse.

The Duke later visited the headquarters of the area controller and for his benefit we had to fly out over the North Sea in formation, return and make a mock raid on Edinburgh which the controller would endeavour to intercept. The weather was not good so we made a low-level approach and had a fairly hair raising-time flying up and down valleys in formation, with the tops of the mountains on either side covered in cloud. Luckily we did not fly into a dead-end and were not intercepted before thundering at roof-top level over the Area Control Headquarters. On return to base at Drem we were loftily told by the local Ack-Ack that we had all been shot down. When we asked them what height we had been flying at they said 12,000 feet! Once again we wished we were on the other side – it would have been so much easier!

On 26 July we took off in Mitchell FV924 leading a vic of three Mitchells which were under simulated attack from six French Spitfires. The cloud base was low so we could only fly at about 800 feet and and Spitfires played the very devil with us, but more to the point we were forced to cross and re-cross the landing circuits of all the nearby aerodromes and soon the sky was a mass of angry red flares being shot into the air by incensed air traffic controllers. We got a mild rocket for this when we landed but I really do not see what else we could have done as the weather was so bad that we should never had been allowed to do such dangerous flying.

On the last night at Drem Wing Commander C.E.R. Tait took us all into Edinburgh, including the French Spitfire pilots, and we had a celebration. A party of the boys took over a tram and tried to drive it down Princes Street while the wing commander climbed a lamp-post to wave them on, but the locals took a dim view and called in the constabulary who broke up the party.

On 29 July we took off in Mitchell II FU932 to return to Swanton Morley. We formed up into tight formation and did a run over Drem in the traditional manner, and the French Spitfires arrived and gave us the beating up of all time – after which they flew with us as escort before peeling off and returning to their base. It was a most perfect display of flying but very nerve-racking, as the slightest error would have written us all off. The course had been a good one and we now reckoned that we had fighter attacks pretty well buttoned up; so long as we did not get an unlucky hit from flak we felt we would now be all right. How wrong we were was to be cruelly demonstrated the very next day.

As an ex-wireless operator I had become friendly with the station signals officer who was a very keen type, and when, on the first day back at Swanton, we heard that there was to be a sea-sweep for some American airmen just off the Dutch coast we took the opportunity to get permission to test a theory we had discussed for a long time. Briefly, this was the possibility of one aircraft homing on to the signals of another using the excellent radio compass in the Mitchell. It was an ideal aircraft for these sweeps for two other reasons: it had a longer flying endurance than the Boston and a much more powerful radio. At 1340 hours on Friday 30 July we took off in Mitchell II FU932 'Q' for Queenie in company with three No. 88 Squadron Bostons. This was the first operational flight of a Mitchell from No. 226 Squadron. Our crew had been due to go on leave and I was wearing my best service uniform. It was a lovely hot day, so hot that I took off my uniform jacket and hung it up in the navigation compartment alongside my service hat. We had taken an additional gunner with us as an extra pair of eyes, as was the custom on these searches. I cannot remember his name, but he was only nineteen, a skinny youth who had never been on an operation before. As we skimmed in formation over the flat Norfolk countryside I looked down at the silhouettes of our aircraft on the ground below and thought how ugly was the shadow of the Mitchell compared with that of the three graceful Bostons.

Soon we were over the coast and flashing across the water of the North Sea in the direction of Holland. Sergeant N. asked permission to test his guns, and after a short burst reported that only one gun would fire. We did not worry unduly at this information – which shows that it is just as well one cannot see into the future. As we approached the theoretical spot in the North Sea from which we would fan out and start the search we gradually climbed to 500 feet, and for the first and last time on a sea search there dead ahead of us was an American dinghy with three figures in it! We all circled the dinghy and it was soon clearly marked by smoke floats dropped in turn from each aircraft. There was great excitement aboard on sighting survivors for the first time, and each aircraft swooped down and 'shot up' the dinghy. This was standard procedure and was calculated to improve their morale, and later I was in a position to verify that that this was indeed so. The occupants of the dinghy must have been pretty far gone as they showed no interest whatever in the four aircraft swooping just over their heads and did not even give us a wave. As I have said it was a beautiful sunny day without a cloud in the sky and round and round the dinghy we circled back now at 500 feet: three Bostons and one Mitchell. We broke away and climbed higher to call base and give our a sighting report and the location of the dinghy, which I had carefully worked out. Back down to 500 feet we went as soon as our wireless message had been acknowledged, and round and round again. As the smoke markers burned low an aircraft would drop another, and every half hour we would climb up again and transmit for the benefit of the other Mitchell that was on its way to relieve us. My log continually read 'Transmitting for bearings' – it never occurred to me that someone else might also be recording those bearings. After about two hours the Bostons had to leave due to shortage of fuel, and after 'shooting up' the dinghy and waggling their wings in salute to us we were left on our own.

It was pretty monotonous going round with the sun beating in through the Perspex, the engines droning, and the endless expanse of sea below. Our orders were quite specific, however: not to return until we were relieved. As each half-hour went by we climbed and transmitted, but as time passed we slowly began to realise that this was not a healthy thing to be doing. The first excitement had worn off and the realities of our situation were coming home to us. I began to give the gunners the bearing of the enemy coast as they must have lost all sense of direction in our ceaseless circling and it would be from the enemy coast that the ominous specks of the fighters must surely first appear. Fuel became a problem and I told Dick that we would soon have to leave; he asked me to work out how long we could remain before we had only enough fuel left to reach the nearest airfield in Britain. The answer was 1750 hours. At 1745 hours exactly I glanced out to starboard through the Perspex of the nose compartment and for a moment my heart seemed to stop.

Riding in perfect formation on our starboard wing tip was an Me410 and beyond that, also in perfect formation, rode three Me210s. (The Me410 was at that time the Germans' latest twin-engined fighter, and the Me210 was no slouch either.) I could see the faces of the German pilots; their heads were turned towards us as they concentrated on formation flying. As soon as I got my breath back I switched on my microphone and reported, 'Four enemy fighters to starboard'. A voice I never identified replied, 'You mean to port', so I looked to port and there on the other wing tip was another Me410 and three Me210s. Nine aircraft, all in perfect formation, one British and eight German, were now going round and round the dinghy!

I can only surmise that the poor turret gunner had dozed off in the heat and that the only reason the Germans had not shot us out of the sky already was that they had never seen a Mitchell before and hoped to take us prisoner so that they could study this new machine at leisure. Be that as it may, I gave Dick the course to steer for base: I will never forget it, it was 240° magnetic. Our chances were nil but I can honestly say that the thought of surrender never crossed my mind. I heard the roar of the engines deepen as Dick opened up the throttles, the nose dropped as we dived towards the sea and turned for home. I unclipped my .303 machine gun in the nose, cocked it and set the safety catch to 'FIRE', but after a few moments realised that our sudden manoeuvre had caused our escort to drop behind and there was nothing for me to fire at. A moment's reflection and I realised that the nose was no place to be, so in record time I slid down the tunnel into the navigation compartment. As soon as I plugged into the intercom I heard Dick's voice saying, 'For God's sake someone tell me which way to turn'.

On each side of the navigation compartment was a Perspex window in the form of a blister just big enough to put your head into and peer out: these blisters were opposite the engines which were only a few feet away. I looked out of the nearest blister, which happened to be the starboard one, and had a perfect view of the leading Me410 which had just peeled off into the attack and looked very pretty with white smoke blowing back from the wings in the sunlight as his cannons fired at us. I told Dick to turn starboard into the attack. This was standard procedure; I also advised him to watch his height over the sea and not to get too low, as fighters corrected errors in their aim by observing the splashes their cannon-shells made in the water around a low-flying aircraft. We banked over very steeply, and the attacking Me410 disappeared from my view, so I crossed the compartment and stuck my head into the other blister. The Me410 was alongside and just above us, and our top gunner had at last woken up. He was lacing away with his single working .5 machine gun at point-blank range and scoring hits all along the enemy's fuselage. I was jumping with joy, but suddenly things started to happen very fast – faster than it takes to describe it. There was a noise that I had heard once before, as though somebody with a big stick was beating the sides of the plane. The engine just in front of my face suddenly emitted dense clouds of brown smoke from under the cowlings to be followed immediately by a whooshing sound, and the smoke turned into a sea of flame.

An aircraft, probably the other Me410, was right on our tail and giving us everything it had got at close range. I switched on my microphone and reported, 'Port engine on fire'; again the voice I never identified replied, 'You mean starboard'. I looked across the compartment and sure enough the other engine was a mass of flame. With both engines on fire and one hundred and fifty miles to go to the English coast you don't have to be a genius to realise that you will never make it, so I closed the armour-plated door leading to the co-pilot's seat and braced my head and back against it so that I was facing the rear. Through the blisters on either side of my compartment I could see that the wing tanks were also alight and sheets of flame, twice the length of the Mitchell, were streaming back from them. The sound of the engines died away as Dick throttled back and I could see the surface of the sea coming closer and closer as we sank down towards it. Suddenly a horrible ripping sound could be heard from the bottom of the fuselage as we touched the water, then I remember looking down at my feet in amazement as the bottom hatch, which opened outwards, burst in towards me and next second I was under water. There was no sensation of water pouring in: one moment I was standing braced with my back against the armoured door, the next I was completely under water. My mind told me that the only way out of the compartment was to unlatch the armoured door and climb up into the co-pilot's seat, above which there was an emergency exit in the roof. I could feel that the Mitchell was sinking to the bottom of the sea. I could not see anything but groped around for the catch: instead I grasped the limp hand of Dick, which must have been hanging down beside his seat. I felt very calm, although later the state of my hands belied this, and even felt surprised that I did not feel short of breath in any way. The door would not budge and it dawned on me that now I must die – there was no other way out of that trap. Having accepted this fact I felt that it would be better to get it over with and deliberately opened my mouth to gulp in water. Suddenly I felt a sort of underwater explosion and sensed myself going up instead of down, only to feel caught and dragged down again. I turned the quick-release knob on my parachute harness and gave it a bang. The harness fell away and I felt myself going up again. My head broke water; the sea was as smooth as a millpond, not a wave, not a ripple, the sun shone and there in front of my eyes, not six feet away, was my service hat floating on the surface. I immediately struck out for it, picked it up and then looked around me. There was oil on the water but no trace of poor old 'Q' for Queenie, only an upturned dinghy with two people swimming frantically towards it. I joined them and after some little difficulty we righted it and climbed aboard, feeling very conscious all the time of the amount of sea under our feet. The other two were Flight Sergeant Bishop, our wireless operator, and the young air gunner. The dinghy was of American pattern, shaped like a boat with two rubber seats and a pair of oars.

The silence was uncanny and seemed to tear at my nerves after the crescendo of sound of a few moments before. I sat on one seat of the dinghy and the other two sat facing me on the other. We all started to talk at once and I quickly shut them up, for I found that to talk of our experiences at that moment only made them all the more vivid. There would be plenty of time for that later and the thing to do now was to concentrate on the present and survival. When I looked down I saw that I had a long tear from knee to thigh in my best trousers, and as I bemoaned this fact the tear flapped open to reveal that I had a large chunk out of both the top and bottom of my leg from which blood was slowly welling. It was only at that moment that I felt the pain! My first act was to comb my hair, put on my cap and straighten my tie, upon which Bishop turned to the young air gunner and said, 'Blimey, he'll turn that end into an officers' mess next!'

On taking stock of our situation we found that the only contents of the dinghy were a knife and a set of wooden stoppers to plug leaks, together with a set of bellows and a pair of paddles. A few objects were floating about in the water and we set out to collect them before they drifted too far apart. In all we collected the aircraft first aid kit, which was useful to bandage my leg, and three individual dinghies; only two of the one-man dinghies held their emergency rations and there was no water. We inflated the dinghies and tied them on to our own dinghy to present a greater area for searching aircraft, and cut out the rubber aprons to use in the main dinghy. We heard the sound of aircraft engines and could see German planes searching up and down. I told everybody to jump out of the dinghy in the event of our being spotted by the Germans and swim in opposite directions. Somehow we all felt that they would not be collecting survivors.

As the sun went down and it gradually became dark our hopes sank too. Suddenly, from the direction of the enemy coast we heard the sound of engines and there coming straight at us at sea level was a twin-engined plane! Just before we plunged over the side Bishop recognised it as a Beaufighter, and sure enough it was. In a chance in a million a lone Beaufighter returning from a low-level sweep over enemy territory had happened upon us. The pilot could not fail to see us as he roared right over our heads, and we were overjoyed to see him climb up into the darkening sky. He circled and we knew he was sending out radio signals to England so that they could locate our position. After a while he came down and the observer's Aldis lamp started to flicker a message. I wrote it down with a pencil on the rubber side of the dinghy. It said 'Have sent for help, must go now, short of petrol, good luck' – and with a last zoom over our heads and a waggle of his wings in salute he was gone. We were left alone again in that endless expanse of sea, but now we were in a much more cheerful frame of mind. Not knowing how long we would be in the dinghy I decided that we had better ration things right from the start, so we had an evening meal of four Horlicks tablets each.

None of us slept that night but by now we felt a little calmer so began to relate our various experiences. Strange to say we all felt very indignant that we had been shot down. We felt that there would be a big fuss when the facts were known that the Germans had been so rotten as to shoot down people on a mercy mission – how young we were. Apparently Bishop had seen poor Norburn, our top gunner, slump in his turret after the first few bursts of fire and he and the little air gunner had tried to drag his body out, but without success. Bishop saw that both engines were on fire and he could hear cannon-shells exploding on the armour-plated bulkhead at the rear of his compartment; some were ricocheting through the sides of the aircraft and he could see that the fuselage was on fire. The little gunner tried to lower the under-turret but it jammed half-way down. Bishop realised that we were not going to make it so he started transmitting. He could not remember the letters SOS so instead transmitted our call sign over and over again; at the same time he stood up with his other hand on the emergency-release handle of the aircraft dinghy. When we hit the sea they were submerged in the same violent way that I was and both were trapped by wreckage as the plane sank, but it broke in half just at that point and they came to the surface.

As the navigator of the party I was continually asked by the other two how far we were from the English coast and when would we be picked up. It has always been a principle of the 'navigators' union' that you never admit to being lost, and this was no exception. At long last morning came and we passed the time anxiously scanning the sky to the west for signs of searching planes – none came. It is difficult to describe how immense the sea appears when viewed from the level of an aircraft dinghy; it stretches away to all horizons, there is sea, more sea and only sea in every direction you look. You are in a world that seems to consist of nothing but water and you feel very conscious of the fact that there is a lot of it directly underneath you too. By noon I had exhausted all the reasons I could think of as to why we had not already been sighted and we all sat in injured silence feeling not a little neglected. At 1330 hours on Saturday 31 July, while many of the good citizens of the British Isles were enjoying a well-earned Bank Holiday, four Beaufighters appeared escorting two Hudsons and – joy of joys – one of the Hudsons had a swollen belly which showed that it was carrying one of the new airborne lifeboats.

The Hudson pilot was obviously taking no chances. First he dropped a smoke float alongside us to show him the wind direction, then he made several dummy runs before finally dropping the boat from a height of 700 feet. Three large parachutes developed simultaneously to hold the boat up and as it swung down towards us there was a loud crack and a rocket line fired from the bows with a drogue attached to keep the boat's head to wind. The boat landed bow first with a slight splash some one hundred yards to one side and slightly downwind to us; the parachutes collapsed and were automatically blown clear; at the same time two more rockets fired and threw out long lengths of floating line, one on either side, so that we could pull ourselves in to the boat as we drifted down towards it. Self-righting chambers fore and aft then blew themselves up! It was a most impressive performance. The Beaufighters now swooped down and thundered over our heads, but we did not need any encouragement and cut free our small dinghies so that we could paddle more quickly towards this very attractive vessel.

We boarded the lifeboat easily enough and had just commenced to slash our old friend the rubber dinghy with a knife so as to sink it when we were all shattered by the sound of cannon fire. When we plucked up courage to look up we saw that it was only our friends the Beaufighters having the time of their lives shooting our small dinghies to ribbons so that they would not give rise to future false sightings. The effect of the sound of cannon fire made me realise that I was still in a fair state of shock. Once they saw us safely into the boat the Hudson sent us a message by Aldis lamp giving a course to steer of 247° magnetic. They then left us to the care of the two Beaufighters which roared noisily around urging us to get under way. It was only now that my theory about air-sea rescue began to come unstuck. During the many lectures we had, both during training and on the squadron, I had always listened with great care up to the point of surviving the crash after which, I had reckoned, one would have all the time in the world to open the various survival packets and read the instructions. What I had not taken into account was the state of shock and the physical condition one might be in at the time which is very different from studying the subject safe and sound in a nice dry hangar. (We had a very good and conscientious air-sea rescue officer on the squadron at this time. He was a flight lieutenant observer and was later shot down, taken prisoner and shot by the Gestapo towards the end of the war in the famous mass prison break.) We had received lectures on the airborne lifeboat and although this was only the sixth one to be dropped we knew that the instruction booklet should be in the starboard engine locker – and sure enough that was where it was.

At this point I think a short description of the airborne lifeboat, as it was at that time, is called for. To begin with, it was not a boat in the true sense. It consisted of a series of watertight compartments which gave it buoyancy, each compartment being fitted with a removable lid secured by wing-nuts. At each end was an inflated rubber canopy which acted both as a shelter and a means of turning the vessel upright if a wave should turn it over. The wooden deck sloped slightly inwards towards a slot which ran right through the bottom of the boat so that it was self-draining; any water that was shipped simply ran out through the centre slot. The sides between each self-righting canopy were lined with rubber foam which had spaces for the oars to be used. Two engines were fitted side by side amidships, each in a separate compartment with their propellers protruding directly underneath them. In addition there were oars, and a mast and sails lashed to the deck. The total length of the boat was about fourteen feet and its width about five feet. As a small illustration of the considerable thought that had been put into its construction I would mention that both self-righting canopies were fitted with an ingenious folding cover, one side of which was a brilliant yellow and the other side a sea blue so that you could hide or reveal yourselves as the occasion demanded.

Sitting in our small craft I avidly studied the instruction booklet while the Beaufighters zoomed impatiently around us. 'First step the mast', it said, which we did after a slight struggle. Reading on I was dismayed to be told, 'Step aerial on top of mast'. Our little air gunner made a valiant attempt to climb the mast to carry out this task but had to give up as he was in danger of going over the side, so the wireless aerial remained unused. 'Next mount the rudder – to do this the rudder and tiller arm fit into a slot in the deck under the aft canopy.' We could not get the rudder into the slot as the tiller arm kept fouling the canopy. In the end we managed but only after having punctured the canopy which collapsed on to the deck in a floppy mess. This was our first setback – but we had the sails up, the rudder in and both engines running. The engines had a flywheel on top and started easily after the first few pulls of a cord wound round the flywheel. I set them to run at half throttle. The engine compartments were dry and we replaced the engine hatches, mounted the small deck compass and I took the tiller and set course 247° magnetic. We made a cracking good speed of around 8 knots and our wake creamed out behind us. The Beaufighters shot us up once more, waggled their wings and were gone.

I had always been very keen on small boat sailing and must confess that I was now thoroughly enjoying myself despite being soaked through and having to sit in discomfort with my injured leg stretched out in front of me. I told the two sergeants to have a rest in the bows under the canopy and this they did, covering themselves with the pieces we had cut from the small dinghies. As the sky darkened the wind, which was from the north-east and therefore blowing from astern, gradually increased. The first hint of trouble came when the reassuring phut phut phut of the engines altered to a coughing splutter and then died away to silence. This roused the crew and we unscrewed the hatch covers over the engines, thinking that they had run out of petrol and would need filling from the spare cans provided. To our amazement we found that both engines had stopped because they were totally immersed in water! On checking the other hatches we found that the forward hatch was also flooded and the first aid kit in there was soaking wet. We pumped out all three hatches with the small handpump provided, lowered the mainsail and set the foresail as the wind was steadily increasing. The rations were moved from the forehatch to one of those aft. The engines refused to start again. The sergeants settled themselves in the bows under cover and I sat at the tiller trying to keep us on course by the fluorescent light of the compass. We were making good progress under foresail but heavy seas were rolling up behind us at a slight angle so that as each roller came up under the stern a hard pull was required on the rudder to keep the boat's head on-course. I have since thought it would have been much better to ride out the storm on the sea anchor, but we had been given a course of 247° magnetic which was taking us home and I was most reluctant to deviate from it.

How long we carried on like this I do not know but the wind became stronger and the seas higher; after one large roller had passed under our stern I gave the usual hard pull on the tiller and it came away in my hand. Instantly all was chaos aboard – we broached and lay across the waves with the top of the mast touching the water and each wave sweeping over us. All loose gear was swept overboard and we hung on grimly in the pitch darkness. I had, as a boy, read many stories of shipwrecks and was quite familiar with what was required. It was essential to get the boat's head into the seas, otherwise we would surely founder. We streamed the drogue and lowered the foresail, all with great difficulty, as we were continually submerged under torrents of roaring water, but this did not seem to make much difference. I decided that we must unship the mast and use it and the sails as a sea anchor. Eventually we succeeded in doing this and, relieved of the weight of the mast and sodden sails, we swung with the bows into the seas and began to ride a lot easier, the waves no longer cascading aboard. The mast and sails were invisible out in the dark storm-tossed waters and all we could see was the drogue line, to which we had fastened them, alternately going slack and then jerking tight. The long hours of the dark night dragged by and then without warning the line parted. We swung back across the seas; the mast and sails had gone

Sergeant Bishop, wireless operator/air gunner (WOp/AG), the author, and Flying Officer Dick Christie, pilot. No. 226 Squadron, Swanton Morley, 1942.

*Dick Christie (left) with Sergeant
Frank Swainson, the crew's first
WOp/AG. Frank was killed in action
during a low-level attack on
Mazingarbe on 31 October 1942.*

The author pictured while flying as an Aircraftsman Wireless Operator in South Africa.

Bostons in formation.

No. 226 Squadron Boston crews who took part in the famous daylight attack on the Philips radio and valve factory at Eindhoven on 7 December 1942.

Bostons attack a target in France during the summer of 1943.

The navigator's compartment in the glazed nose of a Mitchell bomber. The two ball sockets in the Perspex are for fitting a .303in machine gun, stowed by the navigator's right shoulder.

Mitchells of No. 180 Squadron ready for take-off.

Three men in a boat: Flight Sergeant Bishop, Sergeant Lecomber and the author are rescued from their lifeboat by a Royal Naval launch, RML547, after spending three days and twenty-one hours adrift in the North Sea.

The author receives his DFC from King George VI during an open air investiture at Hartford Bridge in May 1944.

Flying Officer Bill O'Connell, the pilot with whom the author crewed-up at No. 21 Squadron, Hunsdon, in November 1943 to fly the Mosquito FBVI.

A Mosquito FBVI at altitude on an air test, with the port propeller blades feathered.

*Bill O'Connell banks
Mosquito FBVI,
HX906, to port over the
River Rhine after
attacking river craft on
a Ranger operation, 10
December 1943.*

*A V1 flying bomb site in
northern France is
attacked from 1,000 feet
with four 500lb bombs by
the author's Mosquito
FBVI, HX950, skippered
by Bill O'Connell, 24
January 1944.*

forever. There followed a period of pure nightmare. We sat huddled together as our little craft plunged first down, down, down, then rose up, up, up, until suddenly a wall of water engulfed us so that we had to hold our breath for what seemed an age before our heads broke to the surface and the whole sequence started over again – all this in pitch darkness with the wind whistling in fury round our frozen, half-clothed bodies.

Eventually, after what seemed an eternity, a faint sign of light on the horizon showed that dawn was approaching. I have never been so grateful for that daily miracle of light. To see the dawn breaking, to know that you had survived through the long hours of darkness, when you thought that you would never see the daylight again, was in itself a heartwarming thing. On this morning, however, daylight only revealed to us how perilous was our position. We were lying across the mountainous seas and although our little craft rose gallantly up the steep sloping side of each wave there came a time, about two-thirds of the way up the slope, when we could see the crest, blown by the wind, curling right over us so that we had to cling on, shut our eyes, hold our breath, and wait until the water engulfed us. When we broke surface we would find that we were looking down into a dizzy valley of menacing green water into which we rapidly slid, only to start the climb up the other side all over again. This went on until time became meaningless and it was just a matter of doggedly hanging on for grim life. It was Sunday, the day before August Bank Holiday! Luckily for us the storm abated that morning and the seas, although rough, had lost much of their fury, so we could take stock of our situation. We three sat huddled together on the port side of the boat which was the only side above water. We had no engines, no rudder, no oars, no masts, and no sails!

The first question that I was asked, and indeed I was asking myself, was can the boat sink? With only one side wholly above water I knew that there was only one way to restore buoyancy and that was to pump out the starboard hatches which were obviously full of water.

To do that the hatch covers would have to be above the surface of the sea and the only way to achieve this would be to let some water into the port-hatches, which would mean losing even more of our precious buoyancy and might make us founder. There was nothing else for it, so gingerly we let water into the port-hatches and slowly the port side of the boat sank lower and the starboard side came up a little. We then stuffed clothing into the spaces for the oars on the sides of the boat and into the sluice in the centre, because by now we were so low in the water that the sea was coming IN through this sluice instead of OUT. There followed about six hours of back-breaking work as we literally baled out for our lives. Luckily the sea was by now only slightly choppy but even so it was most disheartening to see a small wave gleefully slop back over the side as much water as we had just flung out. Slowly, ever so slowly, we gained, and at long last the hatch covers were above water. We could open the flooded hatches and start pumping out. Once this was done the boat rose rapidly in the water so that we could throw all the sodden clothing overboard and open the sluice in the centre.

Rummaging around in the by-now dry hatches we had time to discover more items of equipment, among which was a chart board and a set of sodden charts which I cheerfully threw overboard. More prized items were large waterproof bags containing padded one-piece survival suits with a set of bright yellow waterproofs to wear over them. We each changed into one of these suits and the sensation of sitting in warm clothes was marvellous. I well remember sitting on the edge of the boat and feeling the sheer ecstasy of dry clothing, and not minding a bit as a playful wave splashed over my back – but what was this? A trickle of water was running down my back; the waterproof suits leaked and because they were one-piece all the water finished up in the feet, so in no time at all we were wet, cold and miserable again. Another thing we found was a log for streaming behind the boat to ascertain the speed. We put this to good use by wrapping it in a survival suit and throwing it overboard where it acted as a very efficient drogue for keeping the boat's head into the sea.

That afternoon we were sighted by three Hudsons and we noted with great excitement that one was carrying an airborne lifeboat but apparently the ration was only one per ditched crew because, after circling us a few times, they left. We had discovered a one-inch Verey pistol and a large supply of red distress cartridges which made attracting searching aircraft very much easier. Later in the day three Bostons attracted by our flares circled us until relieved by a third which remained with us until dusk. High seas were still running but we spent another uncomfortable night full of hope as at least our position was now known.

August Bank Holiday, Monday 2 August 1943, opened with high hopes but there was a very choppy sea coupled with a high wind which made a lot of white wavecrests. This must have made spotting us very difficult, as the following brief notes will show.

0730 hours (approx.)	Sighted three Mitchells half a mile away to the south – fired flares, not seen. (To what depths of despair we plunged as the aircraft passed us by I could never hope to describe and what we said about their crews I could never repeat. All I can say is that I hope to God we never passed anyone by on any of the sea searches we carried out.)
1400 hours (approx.)	Sighted by a Mitchell which made several circuits but eventually lost us in spite of our flares. (We could see him slowly going down wind as he went round and round and knew that he had lost sight of us.)
1500 hours (approx.)	Sighted by a Mitchell – same thing happened again!
1800 hours (approx.)	Sighted by a Halifax who stayed with us several hours.
1900 hours (approx.)	Two Hudsons (one coloured white) joined the Halifax, one of the Hudsons remained until dusk after informing us that help was coming. (About time too, we said ungratefully.)

By now we were running very low on distress flares and I decided to keep our last few for a real emergency. We had not been sitting idle all this time, or at least I had not. Always having been a keen messer with engines I had a go at getting ours started. I pumped out the water, removed the plugs, dismantled the carburettors, ran petrol through the pipelines, reassembled the lot and pulled and pulled on the starting cord – but no spark. The magneto was just below the flywheel and without the necessary tools I could not reach it. From time to time we would take it in turns to give the engines a pull but it did no good and only made me realise how weak we were becoming. Since boarding the lifeboat we had rationed ourselves to one pint of water, one tin of condensed milk and nine Horlicks tablets each day divided between the three of us. We all had salt-water sores, and most of mine were on the only side that I could sit on so I could not get comfortable anyway. Our fingers had swollen up like sausages so that we could not close our hands. Our wrists had been rubbed raw by the elasticated cuffs of our yellow suits. The sun had burned our faces a dark brown and we had a fair beard apiece.

That night the other two slept in the bows huddled together for warmth and I sat on the edge of the boat with the one-inch Verey pistol in my hand in case a search vessel passed close by in the night. I was semi-conscious only, and I was very worried about our young air gunner, who had been in a bad way all day and seemed to be slipping away fast; I did not think he could last much longer. The night, as usual, seemed to drag on forever; the wind still blew strongly and in our wet condition this caused much discomfort. I remember thinking how nice it would be to be out of the wind, say sheltering behind a wall near the officers' mess at Swanton Morley. Strange to say it never occurred to me to think of being *in* the mess, that seemed too remote a possibility; just behind a wall would do, out of the wind that seemed to blow unchecked across that endless waste of sea. Suddenly I felt myself falling and with a violent effort just managed to grab the side of the boat before going over backwards into the water. I came out in a cold sweat as I realised that if I had gone over I would have been too weak to get back and that the others were too fast asleep to be wakened by a cry for help. This was my third night without sleep and I realised that I had come to the end of my tether, so I crawled up into the bows, woke Bishop with difficulty, gave him the one-inch pistol and told him to keep watch. I did not remember any more until I awoke suddenly to see that dawn was just breaking. I looked aft and to my horror all I could see was an empty boat; of Bishop there was no sign. My heart was filled with dread that he had fallen over the side as I had nearly done (I think that this was my worst moment as I should never have forgiven myself) and I scrambled hurriedly aft only to find that he was safely asleep under the wreckage of the aft canopy!

At about 0800 hours on Tuesday 3 August three Mitchells sighted us and remained circling for two hours until relieved by a Hudson which was later joined by another Mitchell. Mitchells and Beaufighters then came along and flew over us and went back in a stream over the horizon, returning to repeat the performance all over again. Obviously they were guiding surface vessels to us, and sure enough at 1445 hours two vessels appeared over the horizon steaming straight for us. From our position in the water we thought that they were destroyers but in fact they turned out to be RMLs (Royal Naval motor launches). The nearest launch came alongside with a scrambling net over the side. Sitting in the stern, I was nearest the net and although I was well aware that the captain should be the last to leave the ship I felt that this was no time to stand on ceremony and was helped up the net by many willing hands. In no time we were all aboard and looked after as only the Navy know how. We were kitted out in soft, one-piece survival suits coloured vivid yellow, given a large pair of white seaman's stockings and a pair of white plimsolls. Our boat was taken round to the stern where they tried to hoist it aboard with the boat davits, but it was so waterlogged and heavy that the davits started to bend so they towed it astern. Before this could be done the rope wound round the propellers and the captain, swearing heartily, had to climb over the stern to free it. When the tow started it meant that we could only proceed at about 6 knots.

The RML that picked us up was a Fairmile Class launch with a single funnel, and we were taken to a small box-like structure on the deck which was the sick quarters. On climbing into bed I just lay there and revelled in the delicious feeling of clean dry sheets. To be warm and dry was a luxury that cannot be described. Truly we take the most important things in life for granted. Through the open doorway I could see the stern deck, complete with an Orlikon cannon and our little boat trailing along faithfully behind. The captain came along to see us, wearing a yachting cap (indeed all the crew were dressed more like pirates than naval ratings), and was just in time to stop the cook from killing us with kindness. (He was preparing bacon and eggs for us.) He asked how we were, showed how pleased he was at picking us up ahead of the other ship (they had a great rivalry and painted on the funnel the number of airmen they picked up in much the same way as we painted bombs on the nose of the aircraft to denote its number of operations), and he asked if the crew could have our Mae Wests, as they were not issued with them and prized them greatly. Naturally we said yes. We had been in the sea for three days and twenty-one hours and now felt that our ordeal was over, but in a short while the captain returned to tell us that they had received a wireless message to the effect that there was another crew in a dinghy five miles off the Dutch coast and he was going to pick them up! He seemed very pleased about it, but we were filled with dismay and suggested that we got back into our lifeboat and they could pick us up on their way back. Before the matter went any further another signal came through ordering both boats to return to port immediately. The captain seemed disappointed but we did not share his feelings. Lying between those wonderful warm dry sheets I began to relax completely for the first time for four days; drowsiness crept over me, and my eyes began to close. Suddenly the klaxons sounded, the engines were opened up to their full 20 knots and our poor little lifeboat looked like a surfboard behind us. A sailor dashed into our sick bay and asked Bishop to come out and identify the aircraft circling us. I lay there rigid as I heard him say 'It's a Ju88', and I stared fascinated at the Oerlikon gunner on the stern as he followed the Ju 88 round. I have never felt so helpless in my life. I slid lower into my bed and before pulling the sheets higher raised a feeble hand to tap the nearside bulkhead to reassure myself that it was armour plated – it was plywood! Luckily after a few spasmodic bursts by both sides honour was satisfied and the attack was not pressed home.* The Ju88 flew away, and we reduced speed and continued on our way. I slept well that night.

Next day, I felt fit enough to get up and hobble about. The crew were kindness itself and we learned that they were a scratch crew who had been called out from cinemas or wherever they were spending the evening to take to sea at short notice to look for us. They dismissed the risk to themselves and their obvious pleasure at having picked us up before the other ship, thereby getting ahead of them in total score, was their main talking-point. I was standing in the tiny wheelhouse as we neared the English coast and could hear the captain discussing with the navigator the fact that they were unsure of their exact position after having been at sea for three days There was, of course, the danger of the inshore minefields. At this time I noticed we were approaching some small fishing boats, so brightly suggested that all their worries could be solved by asking the fishermen our position. This suggestion was received in a very frosty manner and I could see that the Navy much preferred to steam into a minefield rather than admit to fishermen that they were lost! However, a buoy was soon sighted and our position fixed. We all went below after having witnessed an amazing transformation as all the pirates turned into naval officers

---

* I have since met Alan Rowe, the first lieutenant of the naval launch that picked us up, and have read his book *Air Sea Rescue in World War Two*. In the chapter entitled 'A Friendly Foe' he states that the Ju88 flew past at masthead height and the pilot gave a friendly wave! He was probably right.

and ratings preparatory to manning ship to enter harbour. As we came alongside we were eating the long awaited bacon and eggs when an excited sailor burst in to announce that there was a proper reception committee on the quay to welcome us. Not before the last of the bacon and eggs had disappeared did we come on deck to see quite a crowd gathered, among which could be seen not a little gold braid and 'scrambled eggs'. After saying farewell to our rescuers we crossed the gangplank to the quay and as we were doing so I heard somebody in the crowd say 'Cor, they are Yanks'. This annoyed me very much so I plonked my battered sea-stained service hat firmly on my head.

We had landed at Grimsby and the first thing that we noticed was that the ground would not keep still but gently rocked back and forth. It was a most unpleasant sensation which lasted for another two days. An ambulance took us to a heavy bomber squadron just outside Grimsby and we were deposited at sick quarters. My two companions were soon disposed of but my leg took a little longer, and while a sick bay attendant dabbed my festering wounds with cotton wool soaked in antiseptic a big, fat, white-faced, medical officer lolled in a chair and said 'Tell me all about it, old boy'. Needless to say the 'old boy' was a little terse. Once this cursory attention was over the ambulance took me to the officers' mess for dinner. I was still clad in my brilliant yellow one-piece suit and a pair of large white plimsolls, my eyes were sunk into my head, my beard was long, I was the colour of an American Indian and altogether I was very conscious of the fact that I must look quite a sight as I pushed open the doors of the ante-room and hobbled in on my own. The effect on the officers waiting for dinner was quite electric – I could have been a being from another planet, and indeed felt rather like one! Once they had got over the shock everybody was very kind but it was funny to watch the effect of my appearance on the later arrivals.

Next morning a Mitchell arrived from Swanton Morley bringing the station navigation officer, who had most thoughtfully brought my spare uniform, shirt, collar, socks and underclothes; he even brought an ounce of my favourite tobacco. He forgot cuff-links, collar studs, braces and a pipe! Many people offered me the use of a razor but I was reluctant to part with my beard. We flew back to Swanton Morley and the two sergeants were sent on survivors' leave but I had to spend two days undergoing intensive questioning from a team of Air Ministry air-sea rescue experts. They went into every technical aspect and were most interested in all the difficulties we had experienced with the various items of equipment. Eventually I was able to go off on leave. My leg was troubling me a lot as I could not bend it, and was worried that it would be permanently stiff. My father had finished his life as a cripple due to an accident at sea and I knew from first-hand experience how this could change a man's life. The train from London to Liverpool was crowded and I had to spend the whole journey standing in a corridor on one leg. At no point on this journey did anyone offer me so much as a helping hand.

It seemed strange to read the telegram from my station CO: 'Deeply regret to inform you that your son Pilot Officer Arthur Paget Eyton-Jones is missing as a result of air operations of Friday 30th July, 1943. Letter follows, any further information will be immediately communicated to you', and the simple but sincere letter written by my squadron commander. This was inevitably a rather emotional leave. My father had died early on in the war and this added blow had rather knocked my mother for six. All in all I was not at all sorry when my ten days' leave came to an end, but once again as the train pulled out of Liverpool Lime Street station I had a strong presentiment that I would never see it again. This feeling had always occurred at moments of departure but this time it was stronger than ever, and for the first time I knew what a condemned man must feel like. I had never thought that I would survive the war and the fact had not troubled me at all up to now, but as the day seemed to get nearer and nearer I suppose it was inevitable that a certain tension should creep in. I had been on an operational squadron for exactly eleven months to the day when we were shot down, and during that time I had completed thirteen operations. A tour of duty, when I commenced, was fifteen daylight operations. I had lost both the other two members of my original crew and many other close friends besides. I was now a survivor and the carefree fun and thrill had gone out of it all.

Arriving back at Swanton Morley I must admit that I rather basked in the attention I received. Senior officers, who had not bothered to notice me before, came over to hear my story or offer to buy me a drink, and as I hobbled about the station cars stopped to give me a lift. My leg was not healing at all well and our station MO sent me to Norwich Hospital for an x-ray. This revealed that I had still got a strip of aluminium in my leg; when this was removed it healed up fairly quickly. Much to my disgust I found that I could not claim for the loss of my best service uniform. I was told by a not unsympathetic adjutant that according to the regulations I should have been wearing battledress and when I enquired meekly about a new pair of shoes he said, 'Sorry but you should have been wearing flying boots'. As a consolation prize he gave me a few clothing coupons which he held for emergency use and this, he said benevolently, was no doubt an emergency. So being shot down cost me something in the region of £25, which was a lot of money in those days.

I had been given a room in the mess which I shared with a pilot. Everyone had assumed that I would now be sent on rest and I must admit that I did not object to the idea, so got rather a shock when I was told quite casually one day that I had been crewed up with a Flight Lieutenant Bill O'Connell DFC, but in the usual way I kept my dismay to myself. Bill was also a Canadian but very different from Dick. He had just returned to the squadron for a second tour of operations and was one of the old hands, tough, strong and as dark as Dick had been fair. He was the deputy flight commander of B Flight. Dick had been friendly and open; Bill was dour and quick-tempered.

On 7 September, Bill asked me if I would like to come with him to ferry a Boston IIIA to No. 88 Squadron at Hartford Bridge. I climbed into the nose and at 1430 hours we took off. I gave Bill a course to steer for the airfield and noticed that he did not keep to it. After a while I switched my microphone on and gave Bill an alteration of course; he neither replied nor changed to the new course. I was furious and sat in the nose in a fine rage. The fact that we did eventually get to Hartford Bridge did not escape my notice and did nothing to soothe my temper. This was a very different pilot from poor old Dick. He would never have known which way to go to get to Hartford Bridge in the first place; that was my job and he would have left it to me without question. This fellow was a very different kettle of fish; he did not need me and, by crickey, I did not need him. All this quite took away from me any thoughts that this was my first fight as an observer after having been shot down, and when we landed I could not get to Bill quickly enough to tell him how I felt. Much to my surprise Bill was also in a raging temper and demanded to know what I had been doing! It soon transpired that the cause of all the fuss was the fact that, unknown to either of us, the intercom was not working. After Bill had seen some of his friends on No. 88 Squadron we returned to Swanton Morley in a Mitchell flown down to collect us. For a first trip as a crew it had not been a great success but I think it made us both respect each other more, and although it was not the last argument we ever had it cleared the air between us. Ours was to be a rather turbulent partnership.

Shortly after this I woke up one night bathed in perspiration and rambling. My room-mate called the MO and I vaguely remember being taken to the camp sick bay in an ambulance. For three days I was kept in isolation and was pretty ill. On the fourth day I felt well enough to ask the MO what was the matter with me. I had a fair idea that he did not have a clue, as my medicine had been changed every day, and this was confirmed when he was very evasive. As a weak joke I said that at least it could not be yellow fever in view of the special inoculations we had had. Much to my surprise he was also evasive on this point. (Some twenty-four years later I met a man who had served in the RAF and he told me that at about this time a faulty vaccine was used against yellow fever;

many died and many were very ill – he himself had been invalided out through it. How true this was I do not know but it certainly seemed rather a coincidence.) While I was in hospital Bill came to see me and told me that he was going on an operation the next day. For some peculiar reason I felt incensed and demanded to go with him, but this was out of the question.

When I did get out of sick quarters I was as weak as a kitten and only a few days later, on 19 September, I took off in Mitchell II FV929 with Bill and Flight Sergeant Bishop, and another spare gunner on a circus operation to attack the synthetic petrol plant at Leivens in France. Leivens is some forty miles inland from Boulogne and for us it was quite a deep penetration into enemy territory. As Bill was the acting flight commander of B Flight we were leading the second box of six aircraft. Twelve Mitchells formed the attacking force in two boxes of six, and being in the leading aircraft of a box we were tuned into the fighters' frequency, on which we could hear the ground controller in England. This had its disadvantages as it was not very pleasant to hear an impersonal voice telling our fighter escort of some one hundred and twenty Spitfires that eighty-plus bandits were approaching from the north-east, etc. The Mitchell carried a bomb-load of four 1,000 lb bombs and took longer to climb up to our usual height of 11,000 feet. We crossed the enemy coast south of Boulogne and experienced only moderate flak. Navigation was not much of a problem as technically all we had to do was follow the first box. Inland the ground was becoming increasingly obscured by cloud banks which were drifting below us. I had just informed Bill that the target was five minutes away and was slightly over to starboard when he called out urgently that the first box were bombing! Sure enough, the first box had their bomb doors open and even as I watched their bombs cascaded down. For a second I was shattered; was I wrong? My confidence ebbed out of my flying boots. Perhaps I had lost my touch; perhaps I was in an even worse state than I felt? I knew only too well what Bill must be thinking.

There was no time for self-criticism. Already the first box were turning away, so I gave the order 'Bomb doors open', and squatted over my bomb-sight feverishly looking for the target, any target, as small patches of ground appeared through gaps in the cloud. With the bomb-button clutched in my right hand and a load of sudden death just the pressure of my thumb away I had a quick glimpse through a gap in the clouds of a large railway line just to my port, and alongside it a big factory. I gave Bill the order 'Left, left, steady', and just as the factory was sliding down the drift-line on my bomb-sight a large cloud obscured my view. Not to be thwarted I called out 'Bombing, bombing, bombing – bombs gone', and gave a quick press with my thumb. Down tumbled our four 1,000lb bombs together with forty 500 pounders from the other aircraft. Bill turned the formation in a tight bank as I gave the order 'Bomb doors closed', as by now the first box were well on their way home and we had split up the close escort of Spitfires which were trying to protect both boxes. I peered anxiously down at the clouds and left my camera running until the film ran out in the hope that it would show enough ground to enable Intelligence to plot the target. Somebody shouted over the intercom: 'Crikey, look at that fire!' and sure enough there was a huge blaze on the ground that shone right through the cloud bank.

As we approached Boulogne I could see that the first box were going to pass right over the town. Knowing how well defended it was I called Bill up and told him to turn to port to avoid it. Because of the trouble we were still having with the intercom he could not hear properly, so I whipped smartly out of the nose, climbed into the co-pilot's seat and yelled the alteration into his ear. As we turned port I had a grandstand view of the first box just to our starboard getting the full treatment. It was a most beautiful display of shooting, one which it would have done our own ack-ack good to see. The first box literally disappeared in a cloud of black ack-ack bursts, and although they immediately took violent avoiding action and were losing height rapidly down to sea level the black cloud never left them for a minute. Every aircraft in that formation was hit and we did not get a scratch. Their leading observer was the station navigation officer and he did not appreciate my remark in the briefing room afterwards that no doubt he had gone over Boulogne just for old time's sake! As we droned our way back across the Channel reaction set in, and half-way down the tunnel from the nose into the navigation compartment I just lay there for a while drinking in the sweet sound of the engines and revelling in the fact that I was still alive. I patted the metal side of the aircraft lovingly and when I climbed up into the co-pilot's seat there was Bill singing at the top of his voice with his flying helmet off!

At de-briefing I did my best to show the Intelligence people where I thought we had dropped our bombs and much to my relief the leading navigator admitted that he had mistaken the target and had bombed some railway marshalling yards instead. The question was, what had we attacked? All the other crews were talking about the large fire we had created. That evening Lord Haw-Haw, the Nazi radio propagandist, did nothing to improve my frame of mind by announcing that the RAF had been over northern France that afternoon and had dropped bombs on a mental home, killing many of the patients. I was the recipient of many sympathetic glances in the mess that night, and my relations with Bill were a little cool. Luckily for me we received a report from underground sources a few days later that confirmed that we had destroyed a chemical factory that had been the target of the RAF for a long time without previous success. Apparently the French workers had ample warning of our approach and none was injured. From their shelters they had heard us droning overhead and one or two of the braver spirits had looked up in amazement as four 1,000 and forty 500 lb bombs hurtled through thick cloud right into their factory. The devastation was so complete that they went home convinced of the superiority of the RAF. So I achieved my best bombing result when I could not see the target!

About this time I had been promoted to flying officer and also squadron air-sea rescue officer. Needless to say that when the squadron took off on sea searches the bomb bays were so packed with rescue equipment that any survivors sighted would have been so deluged with packages that they would have thought it was Christmas. I was also actively engaged with the station signals officer in experimenting with dropping emergency wireless sets on home-made parachutes. We used to roar in at low level over the airfield and throw these sets out. These experiments came to an abrupt end when, on one trip, the set got tangled up in the main overhead electricity cables and cut the electricity supply to the station for a time.

The squadron used to congregate in the evenings in the Castle Hotel in Norwich and the barmaid there knew us well. Sometimes, if we had the day off, we would drift into the Castle about 6.30 p.m. waiting for the aircrew bus to arrive from Swanton Morley, which it generally did at about 7.15 p.m. Our friend the barmaid would be there wiping the counter and would often greet us with 'I was sorry to hear about poor Mr —— '. You would feel the hair at the back of your neck rising because, despite the fact that Swanton would be completely cut off from the outside world during an operation, this meant that somebody had been killed that day. The crews arriving later would confirm this. She was always right, and how she knew was a mystery. This peculiar ability for bad news to travel fast happened in another way also. Some of the married officers had their wives living nearby and I know of a case when the CO jumped into his car immediately he received the news and tore round to the house, only to be greeted at the door by the tearful wife who knew already! Our own air gunner Flight Sergeant Bishop was married to a WAAF on the station and when we went missing she happened to be in the local town of Dereham; the station were trying to find her without success but she got the news soon enough.

We had a farewell party at the Castle Hotel for Wing Commander Tait, our CO, who was leaving us. An incident happened which, I feel, illustrated to some measure the gradual decline in RAF discipline which was, I suppose, inevitable when combat men are virtually living in peacetime surroundings. The party must have become rather hectic because somebody sent for the provost marshal. In came a flight lieutenant and announced that he was the provost marshal. Somebody asked him how we were to know so he produced his armband from a pocket whereupon he was asked to go back outside, put on his armband and come in again. This he duly did and was received with open arms; somebody announced him in a loud voice, took his hat and pressed a drink into his hand. In the meantime his hat was passed round the room and everyone solemnly emptied their drinks into it. The next day the indignant figure of the provost marshal was again seen at Swanton Morley as he laid a complaint against us with the station commander. This was listened to politely by the group captain and at the end of the tale of woe the station commander said that certainly the squadron officers concerned had acted most shamefully and must pay for a new hat for the provost marshal but, he added, this would mean that the old hat would now become the property of the squadron and he would much appreciate it if it was forwarded to them.

On 23 September we took off in Mitchell FV927 for a circus operation on the power station at Rouen. This operation was remarkable for two reasons, one being that it was the first time I had been the leading navigator and the other, although I did not know it at the time, that it was to be my last operation in Mitchells and with 226 Squadron. Just before we took off the group captain's car came hurtling round the perimeter track and pulled up in front of our aircraft. He got out together with Air Commodore 'Batty' Atcherley. The air commodore had his arm in plaster, a sling round his neck and was not wearing flying kit. (Rumour had it that he broke his arm when flying a captured Italian biplane in the Mediterranean. He decided that he would attempt a deck landing on a nearby aircraft carrier. All would have been well but for the small detail that one of the carrier's lifts happened to be down at the time. Ignoring frantic red Verey lights our gallant air commodore descended rather abruptly down the hole in the deck whereupon, so the story went, the Navy in traditional manner brought the lift up and threw the lot over the side – hence the broken arm.) Much to our surprise the air commodore, who was the senior air staff officer at Group headquarters, climbed aboard our aircraft and settled himself in the co-pilot's seat! Turning to me he asked if I was the observer, and when I replied politely that this was indeed so I was rewarded with a cheery smile and told that he would do his best not to get in my way if anything went wrong! My private opinion, which I kept to myself, was that he would have to move very fast to be out of the aircraft before me.

It did nothing for my peace of mind to know that the first time I was leading navigator I had no less a person than the senior air staff officer to witness my prowess. As we climbed towards the French coast I remembered the words of the briefing officer that the only ack-ack defences at the spot on the coast where we were to go in consisted of a gunnery school, which would not be up to much. As I peered down from 10,000 feet in the nose of the leading Mitchell I saw the winking flashes of light which showed that the heavy guns had opened up on us. A few seconds later our air gunner called out over the intercom: 'Heavy flak dead level with us astern and creeping up'. Bill held the formation steady for a few seconds then made a steep turn to port. Glancing out to starboard I saw the ominous black puffs march steadily alongside just where we would have been if Bill had not altered course – obviously it was the instructors and not the pupils who were manning the guns this morning. Rouen soon came in sight, easy to recognise as it lies on the winding banks of a large river. We made our run towards it to baffle the flak and indeed the plan worked because they threw a box barrage over the town; consequently we were not troubled when we did a steep turn to starboard to run in on the power station which was on the port side of the river. I gave what I thought was a good bombing run but was very disappointed to see all our bombs burst on the other side of the river, and it was no consolation to see that those of the second box did exactly the same. We were not troubled by enemy fighters on this trip and although I thoroughly enjoyed being the person responsible for the course flown by twelve Mitchells and some one hundred and fifty Spitfires I wished that the bombing results had been better. On reaching base I came back into the navigation compartment and the great man asked me how the bombing had been but I pretended not to understand – coward! After de-briefing Bill confided in me that the air commodore had nearly driven him crackers. He had been like a schoolboy on an outing; just before we reached the target he had nudged Bill and, pointing over the side, said he had been in charge of a town we were flying over in the First World War! I do not think these great characters of the RAF really knew the meaning of fear. Most of them had done such a lot of flying and had had so many narrow escapes that they now regarded themselves as indestructible. No doubt some of them, when they died, had very surprised looks on their faces.

This trip confirmed how very different Bill was from Dick Christie. Dick would have shrugged his shoulders over the bombing results and left it at that, but not so Bill. We went over the whole thing together time and time again and also simulated the attack on the bombing range until we discovered that the cause of the error had been a lag in the artificial horizon, the instrument by which the pilot keeps the plane level during the bombing run. After a steep turn to starboard such as we had done the instrument showed a false level for several vital seconds afterwards.

October was spent formation flying and on the bombing range, broken by a trip to Bicester, and one to Wittering. At the time I thought that Bill was just calling on old friends and certainly he seemed to have plenty; later I was to know better. Being a flight commander he could authorise his own flights, and it was not uncommon for senior officers to fly to another station to look up old friends. I felt a bit out of it and although enjoying the fact that I was now one of the squadron's senior observers missed my old crew very much.

Once again, as so often in life, once the goal is achieved the snags appear. Towards the end of October Bill asked me if I would like to go with him to No. 21 Squadron to fly in the Mk VI Mosquitos, the fighter/bomber version. I was by now so slap-happy that I think that if he had asked me to ride camels in the desert I would have said yes, so on 25 October I said goodbye to No. 226 Squadron, Swanton Morley, and arrived at No. 21 Squadron, Sculthorpe – a mere twenty miles north-west of Swanton Morley. Before we left the squadron we threw a party, for which Bill and I shared the cost. I don't remember much about it except that I was not in a very festive mood. I had been at Swanton for almost fourteen months; it held many happy and many sad memories for me. Speeches were made by senior members of the squadron to the effect that they were sorry to be losing Bill, while I drank morosely in a corner. Then I noticed some nudging and whispering going on and lo and behold someone got up to say how sorry they were to be losing me and what a rough time I had had on the squadron. I am ashamed to say that when called on for a speech mine was rather acid.

CHAPTER 7

No. 21 Squadron – Mk VI Mosquitos

Geographically the move was not a big one but the atmosphere and conditions of the two stations were vastly different. Sculthorpe, which later became a vast American base, was a bleak, windswept collection of Nissen huts, very unlike the cosy permanent buildings of Swanton. The mess was such a cold place that on early breakfasts I had great difficulty holding a knife and fork! Bill had dropped a rank in the move and was now a flying officer, but even so he managed to wangle a room for himself. I was in a large Nissen hut and as I unpacked my things the other occupants of the room gathered around and started to ask what were, to me, the most unusual questions. The first was the rank of my pilot, the second how many medals he had. I replied that he was a flying officer and had the DFC and bar, to which there were hoots of laughter and I was told that we would undoubtedly be tailend charlie, i.e. the junior crew. This was a surprise, but as I got to know the squadron better I saw the reason for it. No. 21 Squadron was one of the three Mosquito squadrons forming a Wing which in turn was part of the newly formed 2nd Tactical Air Force. The Wing had been raised by Group Captain Pickard, who was well known as the bomber pilot in a wartime film called *Target for Tonight*. He had toured the squadrons of No. 2 Group and talked all the senior pilots into joining his little band. As a result I had never before seen such a collection of rank and medals in my life and the prophets had indeed been correct; a mere flying officer DFC and bar was very small beer. This did not worry me at all as I had a new trade to master. The Mosquito was

fitted with that new aid to navigation, the Gee set, and I had to learn
how to use it. While Bill was studying the flying technique of the
Mosquito I went back to school. As most of the squadron navigators
had also to learn this new art we had our own Oxford aircraft on the
station (the Oxford was a twin-engined trainer very like the Anson
but slightly smaller, and with the great attraction over the Anson that
the undercarriage was retracted by the pilot and not by hand. On 2
November I had my first flight in Airspeed Oxford No. 431 Gee
fixing. Being an ex-wireless operator I took to this new gadget quite
easily and welcomed the aid it was to render us in low-level
navigation.

Two days later I took off in Mosquito Mk IV HS143 with Bill for
the first time. These IVs were used by the Wing to train the pilots on
this model, which had quite a reputation for swinging on take-off.
The crew-rooms were liberally plastered with cartoons exhorting
pilots to swing on the dance floor but NOT on take-off. This was my
first close look at the famous Mosquito, and after the plushy and
solid fittings of the American Boston and Mitchell I was not very
impressed. It was utilitarian, not to say spartan, in the cockpit and
looked as though it had been put together with Meccano. After my
roomy quarters in the Mitchell it was something of a comedown to
find that I sat beside but slightly behind the pilot in a tiny cockpit so
small that each time I moved I dug him in the ribs. To get in you
had to climb up an expanding ladder on the starboard side and
squeeze through a tiny door. The pilot had to get in first, and on
landing the navigator had to get out before the pilot. To do this you
had to prop the little door open and remove the expanding ladder
from its stowage in the back of the door, expand it and fit it into
slots in the doorway, then collect all your gear and climb out. As Bill
was not the most patient of people this often led to heated rows.

On this first flight, I strapped myself in and Bill taxied to the end of
the runway. At the time workmen were fitting night landing lights and
there was a row of them on either side of the runway. Bill opened up
the engines, took off the brakes and we were away. As we gained

speed we swung to port so Bill opened up the port engine to full power, over we went to starboard, so full power on the starboard engine and back we swung to port – and Bill juggled with the throttles once again. As they heard the alternate roaring of the engines the two lines of workmen straightened up as one man and I could see their white faces turned towards us. With alternate engines roaring like a beast in pain we weaved up the runway until they turned and ran in two desperate lines. By this time I had given up all pretence of a casual approach and with a total disregard for Bill's finer feelings as a pilot I had my feet braced up on the instrument panel and my eyes tightly closed. When I opened them we had somehow managed to stagger into the air and Bill was going through what was always a trying time in a Mosquito, that of getting the undercarriage up. I think that the real contrast between British and American aircraft of that time can be illustrated by their undercarriages. In the Boston and Mitchell you just had to select the lever up or down almost irrespective of the speed at which you were flying and forget about it. A most reassuring set of thuds told you that the wheels had dropped into place, but on the Mosquito you selected the lever up and the wheels came up sluggishly, only for one to drop forlornly down again until you held the lever up manually to get additional pressure and watched anxiously until the green lights on the instrument panel showed that they were safely locked in position. Obviously no unnecessary equipment had gone into their manufacture. Take-off in the Mosquito was also very uninspiring: there was none of the violent acceleration of the Boston which pressed you back into your seat, indeed you only just seemed to stagger into the air. Once airborne with the wheels safely tucked away, however, it was a very different story and Bill proceeded to put the aircraft through its paces in a manner which I thoroughly detested as I have never liked aerobatics. We finished up with a low-level beat-up of the mess at Swanton Morley which was quite something!

Bill soon got the hang of the Mosquito. He had been given the wrong gen. about take-off: in actual fact the rudder controlled any tendency to swing much better than the engines. I carried on with my Gee training. As we were now a crew of two my role had changed. No longer did I drop the bombs; this was done by the pilot, and all I had to do was navigate. For this task I had a Gee set mounted just behind the pilot's armour-plated shield; it was fitted with a mask to screen out the daylight and looked very much like a novel 'What the Butler Saw'. My only other aid was a drift-sight mounted on rails near my feet which could be slid out through a hole in the fuselage and was operated on hands and knees (I only used it once). I had no map table and any effort even to fold a map caused loud complaints from Bill. On operations we used a knee-pad strapped on the right knee for a log. I also missed the excellent visibility of our previous aircraft, as I could no longer look directly downwards.

The Mosquito Mk VI carried four 500 lb bombs, two in the bomb bay and one under each wing; in addition there were four .303 Browning machine guns mounted in the nose and four 20-mm cannon which had their breaches under the cockpit floorboards. I found that when Bill was firing the machine guns the cockpit filled with dense fumes, so much so that we had to use our oxygen masks; when he fired the cannons the floor and whole aircraft vibrated so much it felt as though it was going to fall to pieces. Bill loved to fire the guns and became a very good shot. Talking about the cannons, it may not be generally known that these were always fitted with caps over the muzzles, and the armourers had to ensure that the first six shells in the belt were armour piercing so that they would blow the caps off. If, by mistake, the first shells were high explosive they would blow more than the caps off!

Despite the small number of aircrew in the mess (as there were only two in a crew) there was not much of a squadron spirit. This was probably because we were really a collection of individuals; most of us had come from other squadrons and had not yet settled down as a team. We had plenty of low-level bombing practice at which Bill was very good, low-level formation flying and some very enjoyable low-level cross-country individual flights in which we would fly from

Norfolk right across Wales out into the Irish Sea, down to the Scilly Isles, back, still at low level, over southern England home to Norfolk, all in three hours and twenty minutes! The Mosquito cruised at about 280 m.p.h. at low level and was flat out at 366 m.p.h., which was pretty fast in those days. She would fly easily at 240 m.p.h. on one engine and was completely manoeuvrable; it was even possible to do quite steep turns into the dud engine. Sometimes we used to go up and formate on the leader of an American bomber formation, wait until they were all watching, switch off one engine, feather the propeller, then pull away from them, still on one engine.

News reached us from Swanton Morley that the two members of our old crew had both been killed. Bill and I were very upset by the news as we had managed to get them fixed up as part of the new flight commander's crew and thought that they would be pretty safe with him, but apparently their aircraft, which was loaded with time-delay bombs, blew up half-way out to the target in mid-Channel.

Bill was getting rather restless due to the lack of operations and would sometimes take to his bed for two days at a time, neither eating nor drinking anything. If our names were down for a training flight our flight commander, Squadron Leader Ritchie, another Canadian, would chase me off on a bicycle to find Bill, but all he would say was 'Are we on ops?' and when I said no he would tell me to go to hell! He always got away with it. One day we were on a very early morning low-level practice bombing trip and for once Bill had decided to get up. We were the first on the range and the air was very still so that after a quick couple of runs the target was completely obscured by the smoke from the bombs we had dropped. As Bill was doing a steep turn at ground level for our next run in I glanced over my shoulder and saw a stream of red distress flares coming up from one of the control towers on the range. For a dreadful moment I wondered if we had mistaken the other control tower for the target, so back we went to base. It appeared that we had caught the staff unawares and the poor range sergeant was repairing the target when we came in to attack it! Luckily he did not suffer injury, but nearly suffocated in the smoke. This reminds me of a story I heard about a certain squadron which visited a bombing range. All the aircrew were wandering about the range picking up fragments and staring at bomb craters when an aircraft came overhead and started bombing. Without a word being spoken everyone rushed to the centre of the range and stood on the target. They knew from experience that this was the safest place! Once we took off with another Mosquito to practise attacking each other and I was surprised to find, as we did tight turns around each other to get into an attacking position, that Bill, the better pilot, was going to succeed and that the outcome was inevitable. Sure enough, twist and turn as he would, the other Mosquito slowly came into our sights. What shook me was that it took all of five minutes, and the feelings of a crew in actual combat in these circumstances could well be imagined as they slowly realised that they had had it! My seat had an armour-plated back but to give me a better view to the rear the top half could be hinged down, and in fact I never had it up. During a tight turn it felt as though a giant hand was pulling at your throat and gradually it would become impossible to speak, you would be pressed down into your seat unable to move hand or foot, and in the few seconds before you blacked out your vision would go as the blood drained from your head. Luckily as Bill passed out the Mosquito would pull out of the turn and you would both quickly come to, but I never liked the feeling much.

On 19 November at 2000 hours Bill and I took off in Mosquito HP955 on our one and only night cross-country. Bill was about my equal on night vision, that is to say nil, and my first reaction when he opened up the throttles for take-off was that both engines were on fire. At night the exhausts glowed red hot and great tongues of flame, which were completely invisible by day, leapt out of them. I navigated my way round by using the Gee box without once looking outside the cockpit, and when we landed Bill turned to starboard off the runway. After a moment I thought I could see something looming up ahead so called on him to stop. He did so, peered out and could see nothing but I insisted so, grumbling profusely, Bill switched off the engines and we climbed out to have a look. Sure enough, about three feet in front of the starboard propeller was a big unlit floodlamp, and just on the other side of the aircraft was a deep ditch. We had turned off the runway too soon so we had to climb back in and call for help to be towed away! The waiting period was not very pleasant as Mosquitos were landing and taking off behind us the whole time.

On 24 November we took off in Mosquito HP848 as reserve aircraft for an operation against a target in southern France. We flew with the squadron down to Exeter, refuelled and accompanied them for twenty minutes across the Channel, but nobody dropped out so we had to turn back. This was just as much a strain as carrying on but of course did not count as an operation, although we did at least have our 'operational egg' for breakfast. I suppose it must seem strange to the youth of today when you say that to sit down in the mess to an 'operational egg' was quite a status symbol. It meant just what it said, that is you had a *fresh* egg with your meal after an operation, and in a way it is a reflection on how hungry and short of food we were as a country that an egg could be so highly prized.

The next day we took off in Mosquito HP848 on our first operation with No. 21 Squadron. It was a low-level attack on the power station at Aube in France. For these operations we flew in pairs and on this occasion we were the number two, flying in echelon starboard on the leader. The term used for this type of attack was 'Ramrod'. Everything went well except for the fact that I had been issued with an American hand-held camera which was pretty bulky. I had been instructed to take as many oblique photographs of the enemy coast as possible. This was, no doubt, as a prelude to invasion planning. Being a dutiful type I took several photographs as we approached the coast, much to Bill's annoyance as it meant that I was frequently digging him in the ribs with my elbow. Our first turning point after crossing the enemy coast was a small railway station of a branch line at Yerville. We flashed over the roof of the station and changed to our new course just as a German gunner on the roof let fly at us. I heard a thud in the starboard engine alongside me and could see glycol streaming out in a white cloud. Bill quickly shut off the engine and feathered the propeller so I asked him if we were going on to the target. He gave me a withering look and asked for a course for home.

We turned to port, giving the station a wide berth. Bill jettisoned our four bombs, fused not to explode, into a field of cows, much to their surprise, and back we came. As we re-crossed the enemy coast, swooping low over the sand-dunes on our one engine we ran right over a nest of machine guns, so low that I could clearly see the flashes from the muzzles of the guns as they tilted them up and blasted away at us. Bill threw our Mosquito all over the place to avoid their fire as we swept out to sea. It was a very nice demonstration of low-level aerobatics on one engine, but made writing on my knee-pad very difficult. When we neared the south coast of England Bill gave a Mayday distress call on the radio and we were given courses to steer to reach Ford aerodrome. It was a nice day, the sun was shining, I had nothing much to do as we were under radar control and as the beautiful white cliffs of southern England came into view I must confess that I got rather chatty and asked Bill if he had ever been to Ford before. In reply he just said 'Shut UP' and in response to my surprised look pointed to the temperature gauges of our good engine – they were well over the danger mark! (I met Bill again a few months ago for the first time in 54 years. On talking about this he revealed that our one remaining engine was barely keeping us airborne, and he had to choose between crash-landing on the enemy's beach, ditching in the sea or trying to make it home – truly ignorance is bliss. He also told me that the engineering officer at Ford stated that our 'good' engine had, at most, another five minutes' flying time left.) I sat there in subdued silence as the Ford controller brought us in to land in a masterly and cool manner. On touching down he asked us, in a matter-of-fact way, if we would mind trying to clear the runway, so Bill opened up our one engine and we bumped on to the grass.

When we climbed out we had a good look at our damaged engine on which the sump had been shattered by a direct hit with a cannon-shell and as a consolation I took a photograph of Bill standing beside it. In next to no time a Jeep arrived and whisked us off to flying control. On the way we looked in awe at the mounds of crashed aircraft which littered the aerodrome. There were Fortresses, Liberators, Lancasters, Wellingtons, Halifaxes, Stirlings, Thunderbolts, Spitfires and Hurricanes, to name a few. It cut us down to size and when we reached flying control we walked in just in time to hear a loudspeaker requesting the emergency landing at Ford of forty Thunderbolts that were running short of fuel. No wonder our arrival did not cause so much as a ripple. We had to stay the night at Ford and next day an Oxford from Sculthorpe flew down to pick us up. As we landed back at Sculthorpe a Mosquito flew overhead on one engine and I turned to Bill and said scornfully, 'It's all right flying on one engine for practice', but when we got to the mess we found out that it had been our flight commander, Squadron Leader Ritchie, we had seen. He had lost an engine on an operation, his observer had baled out and been picked up safely and the aircraft had crashed near Kings Lynn. While we were in the bar discussing who the new flight commander would be in hobbled Ritchie. He had baled out at about 800 feet, and apart from a twisted knee was all right. I lugged my camera along to the photographic section to get the film developed. Calling in later in the day to see the film I was told that the shutter had jammed open on the first exposure and all the film was ruined! I never carried one of these cameras again.

On 29 November we took off in Mosquito HX976 as the number two on a low-level attack on Cleve in Holland. This involved a long crossing of the North Sea of some one hundred and sixty miles. As 1° off-course puts you a mile out in sixty and Gee reception in the area was poor at the time it was a difficult piece of navigation. The Dutch coast at the point of our landfall was very flat and heavily defended, and it was essential to cross the coast with pin-point accuracy to avoid the most heavily defended areas. We made a bad landfall at Ijmuiden which was a 'hot spot' and returned to base without having actually crossed the coast. This did not please Bill at all.

The next day we took off again, this time in Mosquito HX961, and we were leading. Bill was determined that we should show them how to do things so I spent the long sea trip taking frequent drift readings to ensure we kept on track. In echelon starboard rode two other Mosquitos keeping formation on us. There were no visible landmarks on the flat enemy coast but about five miles inland we should cross the bend of a single-track railway line which would give us an excellent navigational check. The low-lying, menacing coast loomed up ahead all too soon and as we opened up our engines to full throttle and raced across the wave-tops towards it I saw the large frame of a radar aerial straight ahead. This was a bad sign as it was bound to be defended, and sure enough there was a gun-pit at the base firing away at us like mad. Bill was in his element and opened up with both cannon and machine guns, completely destroying the gun-pit. He followed this up with strikes on the aerial just before we zoomed over the top of it. Our cannon-shells looked very pretty exploding on the target just like a lot of twinkling fairy-lights The only thing which spoiled the illusion was the bits and pieces which flew into the air from the target. Then all hell broke loose. Guns were firing at us from all directions, we were firing back and ducking and weaving at the same time. Our other two aircraft were doing the same thing, and what with the cordite smoke and the juddering of the cannons firing it was impossible to tell whether we were being hit or not. Suddenly we roared over a broad main road bordering a canal which had a large double-track railway on its other bank. According to my map there was not a feature like this anywhere near our track – I was lost. (This episode illustrates, I feel, the big difference between an observer and a pilot. There we were sitting side by side; Bill was acutely aware of, and was reacting to, the events happening around us, but I had to ignore all this and instead concentrate on what was to me purely a navigational problem.) I told

Bill for the first and last time that I was lost and that we would have to abandon the operation. He was furious and among all that chaos a terrific argument developed in the cockpit, ending in my throwing my maps on the floor and telling him to find his own way to the target if he was that clever. At this Bill pulled round in a vicious tight turn to port with the other two Mossies faithfully following and we shot our way out through that most unfriendly strip of coast. The passage back across the North Sea was performed in a stony silence and I sat there miserably wondering what had gone wrong. As we touched down, still with our bomb-load on board, we suddenly veered off to one side and skidded across the grass in a beautiful ground loop ending up facing the way we had come. A tyre had been shot off but luckily the grass was very wet and we had skidded, otherwise the undercarriage would have collapsed. I climbed out followed by Bill who, with a mighty heave, threw his parachute as far as he could and walked away without a word, not to the briefing room but back to bed! It was no help to me when the other two navigators asked me in the briefing room why we had turned back, and it was obvious that they had not even realised that we were not in the right place. This time I resolved to get to the bottom of the mystery, and after a lot of hard work discovered that all our Mosquitos suffered from a compass error caused by the fact that the compasses had been checked with the tail-wheel on the ground when they should have been checked with the tail-wheel up in the air on a trestle to simulate the actual flying attitude of the aircraft. The difference gave an error of up to 5° on an east and west heading such as we had flown to Holland, and accounted for our bad landfall. We observers had to get busy re-checking all the squadron aircraft's compasses. Bill was only slightly mollified when he heard the news but at least we were on speaking terms again. What was upsetting him was the fact that we had now completed three operations on Mosquitos, all of which had been unsuccessful. I have since checked up and if we had carried on we would have flown straight across Schipol aerodrome, at the time a main German fighter base.

On 6 December we took off in Mosquito LR292 for a low-level attack on shipping on the Rhine. We were to make a landfall at Vlieland and then run down the length of the Zuider Zee before turning inland to strike the Rhine and attack all shipping on a ten mile stretch, ending up at the bridge at Nijmegen. We decided that if there was no shipping on that part of the Rhine we would blow up the bridge. At Vlieland we ran into dense fog and the operation had to be abandoned. We returned to Sculthorpe in a very gloomy mood. This was our fourth operation that had failed. It is difficult to express how I felt at this time. I had no wish to be a hero and certainly could not claim to be urged on by an overwhelming hate of the enemy, but I had a strong sense of professional pride, call it what you will, which made me feel very depressed by our miserable failures.

The next few days were spent testing aircraft, in which I see undercarriage tests figured prominently. A member of our groundcrew was happy to point out to me that the shell which had blown off a tyre on our last trip would have hit me in the seat of my pants if the tyre had not stopped it. I felt duly grateful to the tyre. Finally on 10 December we took off in a Mosquito Mk VI as the lead aircraft of a pair, to attack shipping on the Rhine in the same manner as for our previous abortive attempt.

This time we flew out as a formation of six aircraft to Vlieland at which point we split up. Two aircraft turned to port to attack another target (they were never heard of again), and two turned to starboard to attack a target in Holland (one got back), while we went straight on over the great embankment holding the sea back from the Zuider Zee. As we crossed this great man-made lake we encountered several German flak ships that squirted viciously away at us, but we turned inland and soon saw the mighty Rhine ahead. Tied up by the shore just ahead of us was a large ocean-going tug and Bill sank it with some lovely shooting with his cannon; then we banked steeply to starboard and started our run. The next two minutes were very hectic as both aircraft swooped and twisted to get at their victims and sometimes we narrowly missed colliding with each other. Bill was having the time of his life with both cannon and machine guns and I had to yell at him to remember to drop the bombs as well. There was considerable light flak in the area but we were not hit. Luckily when we reached the bridge at the end of our patrol we had run out of bombs and behind us lay an assortment of smoking and sunken vessels. On the way back to the Zuider Zee, still at ground level, Bill spied a clumsy He111 flying unsuspectingly towards Germany 1,000 feet above us, and despite my protests he pulled back on the stick and climbed up towards its exposed belly. It took no evasive action but when Bill got within shooting distance and pressed his firing button there was no response – we had run out of ammunition! So we hurtled past and set course for home. The last I saw of the He111 was as it took violent evasive action into the distance; no doubt we at least gave the German crew a nasty scare. As we left the Dutch coast and eased back to cruising speed I glanced out to starboard and saw about forty single-engined fighters flying low over the sea on an interception course. Not being any good at aircraft recognition I nudged Bill, who was an expert, and pointed, speechless. He assured me that they were Spitfires and I sank back into my seat relaxed until I noticed that Bill had pushed the throttles steadily forward so that we were going flat out again. They did not catch us up so I never found out whether he was right or not.

This operation had been a great success and bucked Bill and me up very much. The news soon spread around the squadron, who were also feeling their lack of success, and when the photographs that I had taken were printed that clinched the matter. We spent the next week practising shallow dive-bombing as it was obvious that Bill did not need any practice at shooting. About this time Group Captain Pickard held one of his famous 'Dining-in Nights'. These occasions were bitterly resented by the aircrews who did not like being confined to camp. Our mess was a Nissen hut of the standard pattern. Pickard stood in the centre of the room holding court, a pint mug in one hand, his golden hair flowing so that he looked (and no doubt felt) like some ancient Norse warrior. A small band were playing in the corner of the room and when they stopped for a breather Pickard would turn round and bellow 'PLAY' in a mighty voice. I had occasion to slip out for a while and when I returned I was surprised to see that all the windows were wide open with the curtains drawn back and the light streaming out in all directions! Inside was a shambles: the room was filled with smoke and above all the din could be heard P. bellowing, 'The next person who does that will be put on a charge!' – followed by a loud explosion and more clouds of smoke. Some daring bods had climbed on to the roof and were dropping Verey cartridges down the stovepipes.

The war now took a turn which affected us very much. Our group commander, Air-Vice Marshall Basil Embry, came down to see us. He was a small man but had a big record: he had been shot down twice and captured by the Germans but had escaped, killing two guards the second time, so he was due to be shot if they got their hands on him again. This did not stop him from flying operationally, which he did under the assumed name of Wing Commander Smith. He came to tell us that he had just attended a meeting of the War Cabinet and then showed us a model of the top secret flying bomb sites in the Pas de Calais area. He informed us that he had protested that these sites were not suitable for attack by No. 2 Group aircraft but the order was that they had to be destroyed 'at all costs'. When he said the 'at all costs' bit he looked at us with his piercing steel-blue eyes in a manner that I shall never forget. Those eyes bored right through us so that, although feeling like a condemned man, one would not for a moment consider the possibility of so much as a mild protest. Of such stuff, no doubt, are great leaders made. Not being a man of mere words Wing Commander 'Smith' was the leading one on the Battle Order with Air Commodore Atcherly, the senior air staff officer, as his navigator. This led a wag to burst into the ante-room, shortly after the first Battle Order was put on the notice-board, and announce to all and sundry, 'Have you seen the Battle Order? The King is flying No. 1 and Churchill is his bloody navigator!' True enough, our group commander had a noble following of group captains and wing commanders and I suppose we should have counted ourselves lucky to be included, even though in the rear, on that St Crispin's Day.

We took off in Mosquito Mark VI LR292 on 21 December on the first of many attacks on what were then mysterious targets. Rumour had it that these sites would be very heavily defended and as we knew the area was one of the hottest anyway we were not exactly looking forward to the experience – but we had been clearly told that failure on our part could mean the possible evacuation of the whole of the south of England with the invasion indefinitely delayed as a consequence. As it turned out we were recalled at the French coast because of bad weather and on the return trip our starboard engine packed up so we had to return on one engine. The next day we took off at 0930 hours, this time in Mosquito HX910, to have another go at the same target. Much to my disgust the leading navigator could not establish his position as we approached those sinister white cliffs of France and six of us milled around in a circle just off the coast at 500 feet. I told Bill that I knew where we were and suggested that we took over the lead but he said no, we could not do that. After twenty minutes of this aimless going round in circles (by which time every enemy fighter in northern France must have been alerted) Bill lost his patience and told me to take us in on our own but I was not having any of that so we all returned to base. This was our second attempt to attack the flying bomb sites, referred to as 'Military Installations' as so far the public knew nothing about them, and we had not even seen one.

The urgency with which the destruction of these targets was viewed can be judged from the fact that once again that day at 1530 hours we set off, again in Mosquito HX910, to have another go. This time it was a case of third time lucky, and despite accurate light flak and the fact that we were hit in the tail we attacked the target. The manner in which we were hit illustrates the accuracy of German light flak, brought to a high degree of efficiency by practice no doubt. We were skimming over the fields at our maximum 366 m.p.h. some five hundred yards from the high cliff tops on our way home. On our port side was a dense wood and as we flashed past it we came opposite a square section cut out of the wood in which a light anti-aircraft gun was sited. The gunner was presented with the most difficult shot possible – a right-angle full deflection shot with only seconds in which we were in view but in that time he managed to get off two bursts of tracer, the first of which flashed in front of our windscreen and the second hit us in the tail. Tracer was fascinating to watch: it used to curve, almost lazily, towards you and then would suddenly seem to speed up as it got nearer until it flashed past. Later on the Germans stopped using tracer and I felt worse about this because with tracer at least you knew when you were under fire. Without it you never knew, so tended to imagine it was happening all the time.

The next day we took off in Mosquito HX906, in which we had had such a good trip against shipping on the Rhine, on another attack on a flying bomb site. The pattern of these operations had now settled down to two main types of attack. In the first we used eleven-second delay bombs and went in at 0 feet, and in the second we pulled up to 1,500 feet just before the target and went into a shallow dive to bomb at 1,000 feet, which was the minimum safety height at which 500 lb bombs could be dropped. Even so the force of the explosion used to throw us about a lot and occasional bomb splinters came up through the floor of the aircraft; you could even hear the sound of the explosion over the noise of the engines. Of the two methods of attack the 1,500 feet one was the more accurate owing to the problem of 'skipping' bombs at low level, but it made the aircraft very vulnerable at that height. The flying bomb sites were difficult to attack as there was only one small square concrete building housing the delicate auto-pilots which was worth hitting. The Germans had relied on camouflage to protect these sites and it was very effective. The countryside was dotted with numerous small woods, many of which had farmhouses and outbuildings situated in them and it was in these woods that the Germans had sited their devilish devices, using the farm buildings to house the crews. The wings and fuselages were stored in underground hangars and brought above ground for assembly only just before firing from the small and difficult-to-see ramp which was situated next to the square concrete building in which the auto-pilots were stored; these were fitted last. Often we would attack the wood at the particular corner marked and not until our film was developed would we know whether we had been successful or not. All we had seen were trees, trees and more trees. As I have mentioned before the whole area was most heavily defended and on this occasion we were hit in the port spinner (that is the streamlined cone fitted in front of the propeller) by a burst of machine-gun fire.

On Christmas Eve we took Mosquito HX910, which had been hit in the tail on the 22nd, down to Hatfield for repair. Up to now none of these flying bomb sites had gone into action and the public were quite unaware of what was in store for them. I was feeling quite tired having done four operations in three days – a big change from the days on No. 226 Squadron in which we had often gone for weeks without any sign of action. I was troubled with asthma at this time although, of course, I kept the fact very much to myself, but it usually hit me at night which meant that I was not sleeping very well. Another strange thing was that I had great difficulty in wearing my oxygen mask; normally we used to have it hanging loose on one side of our flying helmets but when things became hectic you had to fasten it across your face so that you could leave your microphone switched on and have both hands free. Each time I fastened it across my mouth it made me retch violently. Nerves no doubt, but annoying. Something else that I found myself doing increasingly was gazing longingly down at some farm worker in a field or some villager walking down his quiet village street as we roared overhead in formation, wishing with all my heart that I could change places with him. There was a dreadful inevitability about our life; from the moment you were on the Battle Order every step, every movement took you nearer and nearer to the moment when you would see guns all round you, each doing its best to blast you out of the sky. It was as though my whole body was rising up in revolt at the way in which it was being constantly subjected to the possibility of imminent destruction.

The year finished in a typically Pickard fashion. On 31 December the whole Wing was to move to Hunsdon, just north of London. This was to be no ordinary move. We were to take off from Sculthorpe, attack flying bomb sites and land at our new base of Hunsdon, so demonstrating to the world at large our extreme mobility. At 1030 hours we took off in Mosquito HX906. If we had been forced to land in France the Germans would have received some very well-equipped prisoners indeed. The parachute section had already left for Hunsdon the day before so none of us had parachutes and had to make do by sitting on our rolled up greatcoats. The back of each aircraft was filled with the personal belongings of each crew; in ours we even had Bill's small radio! We were leading and I well remember the shock Bill gave me when, on crossing the enemy coast, I gave him the next course to steer and he replied that it did not mean a thing! Apparently his instruments had just failed and his gyro compass had toppled so I had to quickly point out a landmark for him to head for, and in this manner we found the target and eventually Hunsdon. On the ground at Hunsdon everything was a shambles. The station had been notified that we were arriving but no one had bothered to tell them that we were doing an operation on the way. The result was that flying control stood by amazed to see Mosquitos coming in on one engine or with damaged undercarriages. Eventually everything was sorted out and we settled in.

Hunsdon was unlike any other station I had ever been on. It had been a fighter station before we arrived and the mess was in a large country house surrounded by woods in which had been erected Nissen huts for us to sleep in. A main road ran through the camp and it was possible for a motorist to stop his car and make a note of the names of the crews called to the operations room by the Tannoy, if he so desired. This did not seem to worry the authorities at all. Another thing that I found unusual about Hunsdon was the fact that we were much nearer large centres of population than I had ever been before. As it turned out I did not get much chance to take advantage of this fact but I was pleased by it, because I was getting very fed up with our communal way of life and sometimes felt a great longing to live in a house once more. Bill and I shared a room and often we would not bother to go to the mess for dinner at night. Being a Canadian he always had a big case full of tins and he used to provide the food and I did the cooking!

Shortly after we arrived at Hunsdon, Group Captain Pickard announced that we were all to take part in an escape exercise. Without further ado we were bundled into aircrew buses and taken out into the country, together with the station photographer. The reason for the presence of the photographer soon became clear. When we arrived at our destination the gallant group captain was mounted on horseback and attending the local hunt; we were to be his admiring aircrew waving him off in a photograph to be published in a glossy magazine. Our disgust turned to dark resentment when the trucks departed, leaving us to find our own way back on a cold and damp day. I have a photograph, taken by the same photographer, of myself and two friends, taken outside the nearest pub shortly afterwards! Needless to say that did not get into a glossy magazine.

One night we held a party on our own in the mess. It was one of the usual affairs and I was carried back to our hut fairly early on by two friends. The next day all hell broke loose. Apparently at the end of the party someone (I found out later that it was Bill) had gone round the mess setting light to the many notices pinned up by our group captain, such as 'Officers will not wear scarves in the mess', or 'Officers will not bring dogs into the mess', all of which would not have been resented if the group captain himself had not worn the longest scarf of all and brought the most enormous beast of a dog into the mess. His lordship had come in late that night and had been greeted with a strong smell of burning and a few pieces of charred paper supported on the notice-board by drawing pins. His reaction had been immediate; all leave on the station was stopped.

We were stunned, as the airmen and airwomen had obviously not been involved and to stop their leave was most unfair. Twelve of us who had been at the party got together and decided we would own up collectively to the 'crime' to get the leave ban lifted. Our party trooped off to the station adjutant's office. We consisted of four squadron leaders, six flight lieutenants and two flying officers, so we felt fairly safe. The adjutant gave our deputation a startled look and fled into the group captain's office; he returned and we were marched into the presence. His lordship lay sprawled back in a chair behind a big desk. Without any preamble whatever he looked at the four squadron leaders and said 'Flight Lieutenants'; then looked at the six flight lieutenants and said 'Station duty officer for a month'; with a frosty look at us two flying officers he said 'Orderly officer for a month', and in a dazed silence we were marched from the room by the adjutant!

The four squadron leaders were old hands and, having friends in Group Headquarters, soon had their 'illegal' sentences quashed. The six flight lieutenants shared a month's station duty officer between them without too much strain. The other flying officer was posted on rest and I was faced with a month's orderly officer. This meant that I was confined to camp for a month, and as a further blow the bar was put out of bounds – but this only meant I had to drink in private as plenty of friends supplied me with the necessary in my room. The news soon spread around the camp and the first few times I appeared in the airmen's dining hall and the orderly sergeant bellowed 'Orderly officer, any complaints?' I received a standing ovation! I used to go on operations wearing my orderly officer's armband with its red letters OO on a black background, and used to remark to Bill that there was no doubt what job I would get if we were ever taken prisoner. The more crafty airmen soon tumbled to the best psychological time to ask for a late pass: when we landed after an operation and taxied to dispersal there would always be a little queue of people patiently waiting, knowing very well that if they came up to me as soon as I wrenched off my flying helmet I would sign anything just to get rid of them.

On the other hand, I warmed to this new task and soon found out a lot about it. Normally one only did orderly officer once in a blue moon, and just adhered strictly to the minimum requirements on the printed sheet issued by the station adjutant. I well remember the face of the supply sergeant when I dropped in on him to sign for the rations for the airmen's mess. 'Just sign here, Sir', he said cheerfully. I enquired politely where the items were and he said, in a surprised manner, that they were already in the 10-ton lorry outside. 'How do you expect me to check them in there?' I enquired. For the first time ever the whole of the rations were unloaded and checked. One morning I received a complaint in the airmen's dining hall that the liver was underdone. Not being a special friend of RAF cooks I gleefully took the complaint up with the sergeant in charge. He was most indignant: 'Underdone', he exclaimed 'underdone!' – and triumphantly pulled out several large trays from under the counter. Each tray was loaded with charred, blackened lumps which presumably had at one time been liver. There was enough ruined liver before me to feed at least one hundred families. The sergeant stood by proudly, but I was lost for words.

Eventually I got myself so organised on this orderly officer business that I managed to talk the motor transport officer into supplying me with a car and driver with which to do my rounds. The first time I used the car, however, was rather unfortunate. It was after dark and my first port of call was the guardroom. I had dressed up in my best uniform, complete with service cap and greatcoat for the occasion, and we pulled up in style outside the guardroom. The driver, entering into the spirit of the thing, jumped out, raced round the car and opened the door for me. I stepped out majestically and the service police outside the guardroom, resplendent in white webbing and gaiters, snapped to attention; their sergeant gave me a sizzling salute which I returned gravely. Then I stepped forward, my feet were jerked from under me and I skidded across the grass to come to rest at the sergeant's feet with my hat rolling away into the darkness! I had not noticed the neat ropes fencing off the grass;

once again my night vision had let me down. In the guardroom at this time they had a prisoner awaiting removal to the glasshouse. I never found out what crime he had committed but he seemed a very mild sort of chap. It was my job last thing each night to visit the prisoner, and more often than not he would be asleep in which case I did not bother him. One night however he was up when I called on my rounds and after the usual enquiry as to his health and well-being there was a pause and he suddenly said, 'I am going to-morrow, Sir' to which I replied that I was sorry. 'I will miss you, Sir', he said, to which I truthfully replied, 'And I will miss you', and in this way two wrongdoers said farewell to each other.

On 14 January 1944 we took off in Mosquito HX906 to attack yet another flying bomb site. We carried a six-hour delayed-action bomb on this trip and landed at Dunsfold on our return owing to poor visibility at base. Our next flight was a week later when we took off in Mosquito HX906 again, on a similar mission. On this occasion we were flying No. 2 on the leader and I must confess that I was sitting back taking life fairly easy when the radio crackled into life and the leader asked us to take over as his Gee set had just packed up. There is all the difference in the world between watching what sort of a job the leading navigator is making of things and actually having to do it yourself!

We carried out a night flying air test lasting thirty minutes on 23 January and the next day at 0900 hours took off in Mosquito HX950 on another flying bomb site mission. Once again we had to land at Dunsfold on our return. The squadron was so committed to operations during this month that there was no time or aircraft available for practice flying. Hunsdon suffered very much from being so near London and at this time of year there was often a thick haze rising up to about 1,000 feet. We would often take off into this haze with practically nil visibility and it was not until we had climbed up through it that we were able to formate on each other. It made map reading to the south coast very difficult. Sitting beside the pilot in a Mosquito the angle of view was very oblique compared with the Bostons and Mitchells, from the nose of which you could see vertically downwards. On the other hand the Gee sets were a big help, and using them you could guarantee making a landfall on the enemy coast to within a few hundred feet of track at 0 feet. Being winter the Channel was often in an angry mood and as we flew over it at wave-top height our windscreens were often coated in salt spray, making visibility very poor. I used to hope we would never have to come down in that icy water; the Mosquito did not have a very good ditching record and only floated for a short while, during which the cockpit was practically immersed. About this time some friends of mine on No. 226 Squadron had to ditch their Mitchell in the Channel. An air-sea rescue boat had been alerted and was alongside within five minutes. All the crew escaped from the Mitchell and boarded the aircraft dinghy but had died of exposure before they could be picked up.

As I have mentioned before Bill was very keen to get out of the aircraft as soon as we landed and in order not to keep him waiting I always used to pack up all my gear as we were approaching the airfield. One day when we were leading the squadron back from an operation I got my head down in the cockpit and started packing my things away. The airfield was dead ahead of us but unknown to me Bill missed it and, much to the surprise of the rest of the squadron, we sailed right on over Hunsdon. When I had finished tidying up I looked out, expecting to see us flying round the circuit ready for landing, but got quite a shock to see we were still flying straight on. This meant that I had to get my map out again and find out where we were. When we eventually landed I received quite a bit of ribbing about trying to get extra operational flying hours in!

My friend, who had his photograph taken with me outside a country pub during our 'escape' exercise, was shot down. He was a quiet, pipe-smoking, thoughtful sort of chap, and much to our surprise turned up some three weeks later. His story was an interesting one. They were hit by light flak over the target and had to make a forced landing on a French beach. The aircraft was practically undamaged so they pressed all the red buttons to explode the destruction charges on the secret equipment, but nothing happened. They then fired the Verey pistol into the cockpit, and nothing happened. In the end they were reduced to climbing on the wings, opening the petrol caps and flinging matches about, but at this stage some German soldiers had arrived and started shooting at them so they were forced to surrender. They then suffered the indignity of having to help the Germans load all the secret equipment into a truck into which they were also bundled and taken to Paris. My friend had hurt his leg slightly during the crash and he had made a great play of this to the Germans. In the truck he quietly removed all his badges of rank and when the truck stopped in Paris and they were told to help unload he promptly took to his heels and bolted round the nearest corner. He was lucky enough to be picked up by the Resistance and back he came. Another crew, a couple of real characters, made a successful forced landing and hid in the centre of a wheatfield. They sat there while the searching Germans burned half the wheatfield and all of a nearby wood. When they had gone our chaps crept out, were picked up by the Resistance and were back with us within a fortnight, complete with snapshots showing them having a lovely time with a party of charming French girls! I was to meet these two later when we were on ferry duties to France. They used to disappear for days at a time and go and meet their Resistance friends, leaving their aircraft at the nearest airfield. In the end they were taken off ferry duties as nobody ever knew when they would be back!

I could not help but reflect during these attacks in the Pas de Calais area how the air war had changed. Over France one never saw a German fighter: the air was full of Allied aircraft and I remember how, one day, we plunged down the side of a mountain, in formation, into a valley – only to run into a cloud of American Thunderbolts which were roaring up the valley. How we missed each other I do not know, but there were aircraft going over and under each other in all directions. Returning to England across the

Channel it often struck me what a sign of the times it was to see all the crews of the aircraft around us happily sitting there without a backward glance at the enemy coast receding behind them. If a German fighter had got among them he would have had a fine old time. Twelve months earlier it was not considered safe to relax until your wheels touched the runway – and even then the odd Me109 might pop up out of nowhere. One day we were flying along at 0 feet and just passing a sleepy French village when, much to our surprise, it suddenly flew into the air in bits and pieces of flame and rubble. Looking up through the Perspex top of our cockpit I could just make out the silvery shapes of hundreds of American Fortresses flying some 20,000 feet above us. Another day we were tearing across a field and heading straight for a raised roadway on which was a farm cart piled high with hay. As we drew near the French farmer rose to his feet and waved wildly at us. Still we came on, I saw his hand freeze into immobility, then just before we pulled up over his cart his nerve broke and he dived head first into the hay!

In the countryside in which we were operating against these flying bomb sites we had come across many strange towers. We had taken these to be flak towers and Bill had acted accordingly. The first time we came across one Bill had opened up with his cannons and I had admired the pretty fairy-light effect of the shells bursting all over the target. Much to my surprise the other two aircraft formating on us took violent evasive action. They had seen the twinkling lights on the tower and taken them to be the muzzle flashes of firing guns and then the smoke from our cannon pouring out of the belly of our aircraft and assumed that we had been hit! One day we mentioned to our senior Intelligence officer, a very nice old First World War squadron leader pilot with only one leg, that we had attacked these towers, and he told us in no uncertain terms to leave them alone as they were water towers. Bill said nothing but on our next trip he opened up at one and kept the plane's nose down so that we barely scraped over the top of the tower. We both looked down then looked at each other. No words were necessary – through gaping holes in the tower water was pouring out! I wonder how many rural Frenchmen reaching up to pull a chain had cause to curse the RAF.

On 25 January we took off in Mosquito HX950 on a low-level attack on a flying bomb site using eleven-second delay bombs. We were leading and clobbered the target well, our aircraft being damaged by light flak in the process. Bill and I had developed a technique for attacking these targets which was paying dividends. I took him to a point about one minute's flying time from the target and turned him on to the heading for it. Before the flight Bill had memorised this run in from an inch-to-the-mile target map, and provided that I got him to the start point he could pick out the target. We did this because we found that at 366 m.p.h. there was no time for me to identify the target and then point it out to Bill before we had shot past it.

Our squadron CO, Wing Commander North, was sent on rest and our new CO was Wing Commander 'Daddy' Dale. He was a charming man, older than most of the pilots. He was a big chap and had a gammy leg which meant that it took two airmen some considerable time to help him into a Mosquito; this was to have tragic results. I often think of him when I meet people these days considerably his junior in age who tell me smugly that, unfortunately, they were too old for the war, or had flat feet or some other condition. Other operations were being carried out by the Wing at this time although I took no part in them, generally being on leave when they took place. They were chiefly 'news' attacks – those that made the headlines – such as the raids on the various Gestapo headquarters in occupied countries. Most of the top brass took part in these attacks, mainly I feel because it was on such raids that the medals were handed out; but I may be unfair at that because many of our top brass had been directly involved with the Resistance and such raids took on a rather personal note. Much has been written about the way medals were issued during the war, and I agree with most of it. I remember after one such raid, the top brass, who had, of course, been leading, came into the bar. Words such as 'Piece of cake' and 'They did not even have the covers off their guns' flowed around; all were in high spirits.

Some twenty minutes later a few white-faced flying officers would quietly slip in and order a drink. The covers had been off the guns by the time they got there.

The chart in the flight commander's office now showed that I had completed thirty operations and was leading the field in this direction and due for a rest, even under the extended tour of duty now in operation. I was told, however, that they were extremely short of leading navigators and would I please do a few more. Bill also wanted me to stay so that he would complete his second tour of twenty-five operations with me – so I stayed. This was not out of any sense of bravery; it was just that I was feeling so flak-happy that nothing much was registering any more. It was considered, not without cause, extremely unlucky to do another operation above your tour and there had been many instances of 'just one more' being just one too many. I was to do another five in the next fortnight. Nobody was more surprised than me that I survived them.

On 29 January we took off in Mosquito LR372 to attack a flying bomb site. The leader was unable to identify the target on the first run in and committed the fatal error of circling the target area at 1,500 feet to try to identify it. Once you commence a circling movement it is very hard to retain your sense of direction and six Mosquitos went round and round in a large circle time and time again. Every now and again an aircraft would peel off with bomb doors open and dive down on some innocent French farmhouse, only to realise his mistake at the last moment and close his bomb doors and climb away, hotly followed by the rest of us. The people below had no idea how close they all were to sudden death. It was a measure of the effectiveness of the German camouflage that although we knew the site was definitely within that circle we never did find it. On the way home we had to cross a small valley. As we swooped down one side of the valley we flew directly over the barrel of an 88 mm heavy anti-aircraft gun which was pointing almost vertically upwards. Although they had only a few seconds' warning the German crew fired, and we were considerably shaken about by the blast as the shell screamed up to some 20,000 feet or so. I hate to think what would have happened if it had hit us.

In the afternoon of the same day at we led a section in an attack in Mosquito HX952 at 0 feet with eleven-second delayed-action bombs. On these raids each section flew at two-minute intervals, and with the whole Wing operating we formed a long line of Mosquitos so that when the first section were crossing the enemy coast the last sections were just leaving the English coast. Once across the enemy coast each section made their own way to the flying bomb site that they had been detailed to attack. As we neared the enemy coast and saw the familiar white cliffs approaching we were rather dismayed to see the section ahead of us wheel about and come back towards us. As they passed overhead we could see that two of them had engines knocked out and the third had considerable wing damage. Evidently there was a hot reception ahead! Our section fanned out into line abreast and we went in with cannon and machine guns blazing. Bill raked the face of the cliffs with fire and we crossed without a scratch. The whole trip was one of intense light flak and we used up all our cannon and machine-gun ammunition. The month closed with a flight in the unit's Oxford aircraft in which for one hour and thirty-five minutes I had to train some new squadron navigators on the Gee set.

On 5 February we took off in Mosquito LR292. Once again we were leading and managed to locate the flying bomb site and hit it accurately, despite the fact that our aircraft was hit several times. About this period we were paid the nicest compliment I ever received in the RAF. Our old friend the one-legged squadron leader Intelligence officer greeted us quite sincerely on return for de-briefing with the statement that we were the one crew for whom he always wrote 'Target Attacked' without even having to ask.

Three days later we took off in Mosquito LR371 on yet another low-level attack on a flying bomb site. As it was an early start our aircraft had been taxied up, nose to tail, at the end of the runway. This was done because the Merlin engines had a great tendency to overheat if run on the ground too long. In the cold grey light of morning in winter I noticed, as I waited at the foot of the ladder for Bill to settle himself, that our groundcrew were acting strangely; they kept grinning bashfully at each other and shifting about, first on one foot and then on the other. At the same time I heard a whirring sound coming from the region of the starboard wingtip. On turning round I found that I was staring straight at a news camera lens. My reaction was instantaneous: I felt outraged. Was there no privacy? Could not a man go to war in peace? I shook my fist at the camera and yelled a heap of abuse before climbing up into the cockpit. When we took off I saw the same fellow at the end of the runway filming us as we got airborne. Again I was filled with rage and opened my window and shook my fist at him. Needless to say I did not appear on the news! No doubt the public would have considered my gestures unfitting for one of our gallant boys about to attack the enemy. On this trip we lost our No. 3. We saw him lag behind as we approached the target and we waited for him just off the French coast, circling round for some ten minutes, but he was never heard of again. My photographs showed him breaking away from the attack and heading for the coast, a mere three minutes' flying time away – which shows that a lot could happen in three minutes. Both Bill and I felt very depressed about this, as we had never lost anybody from our formations before, and in some peculiar way felt responsible.

There was not much time for reflection, however, as at 1510 hours on the same day we led our last low-level attack in No. 21 Squadron. The results were good and the flak only moderate, but I must confess that I approached all these last few operations much as a condemned man must face the walk to the scaffold. I just could not get away from the idea that I had tempted Providence once too often. The relief on getting back left you physically exhausted and it was only then that you realised that your clothes were soaked through with sweat.

In all I had been a member of an operational aircrew for an unbroken period of one and a half years, during which time I had flown 292 hours 55 minutes by day and 2 hours 15 minutes by night, and chalked up some thirty-five daylight operations. We both went on leave for ten days and as Bill was returning to Canada afterwards we said goodbye on Liverpool Street station. It was an awkward moment and as we shook hands Bill thanked me for saving his life by good navigation – this rather surprised me as Bill was not one for compliments – and we parted. You get to know a man very well when flying with him, and Bill was one of the best.

On returning to the squadron after leave the wing commander called me into his office and asked me to check the compasses of the new aircraft coming in. The squadron had suffered a lot of flak damage and the Mosquito, unlike the metal-skinned Bostons and Mitchells, could not have a metal plate riveted over the hole but had to go back to Hatfield for skilled carpenters to insert new panels. The compass check was the only thing holding up the aircraft becoming operational, so I spent a cold and miserable week out on the airfield swinging Mosquito compasses (making sure, of course, that the tails were up on trestles in the correct flying attitude). In return Wing Commander Dale asked me where I would like to be posted on rest – the choice was mine. My answer was simple: anywhere, anywhere at all, so long as it was not in Norfolk, and Swanton Morley in particular. That place had too many memories for me.

On 27 February my posting came through – to No. 1508 Flight, Swanton Morley.

CHAPTER 8

On Rest

Once more I was starting a new phase of my service career on my own. This was a feature of service life which I particularly disliked. You joined a unit, made friends and fitted in – then all at once you were off again and had to start all over. I cannot remember much of the next two months; maybe it was reaction setting in. When I joined No. 1508 Flight, it was commanded by a Flight Lieutenant Osborne who I cannot even vaguely remember. We flew in Airspeed Oxfords on Gee instruction for navigators. I had never liked the Airspeed Oxford very much and liked it less now. It was smaller, slightly faster and more manoeuvrable than the Anson and had a proper hydraulic undercarriage, but even so it was not as nice an aircraft from my point of view. A feature which I disliked was that, for Gee instruction, the cabin windows had been blacked out and a curtain installed across the width of the aircraft so that pupil and instructor sat facing the rear in a blacked-out compartment with only the green flickering tube of the Gee set for company. I often used to emerge from these sessions feeling very much like an owl. Another thing which I disliked was the fact that I no longer had a regular pilot to fly with – I had to fly with anybody. Some were good, some poor and some plain bad. In March I clocked up 63 hours 20 minutes' flying, and in April 64 hours 25 minutes.

April was distinguished by the fact that Squadron Leader Reeve took over as CO. He was a very handsome, tall and gentle man and on 30 April at 1050 hours we took off in Boston IIIA BZ518 to fly to Hartford Bridge. It was very nice to fly in a Boston again. The IIIA was the latest version; the big difference was that the nose had now been fitted with a Perspex bubble instead of, as before,

individual Perspex panels. It gave better visibility but there was a
fair amount of distortion of vision through the more curved
surfaces. At 1345 hours we brought another Boston IIIA, BZ384,
back to Swanton from Hartford Bridge at 0 feet! One of the pilots
that I flew with was Flight Sergeant Lear who had been a pilot on
No. 47 Course with Dick Christie at Upwood OTU. He was a very
nice quiet chap. Another pilot was Warrant Officer Lockman, who
came from Holland. He was one of several pilots flying with us who
had flown flying boats in the Far East and had done wonders
bringing refugees out as the Japs advanced. They were old as pilots
went in those days but were wonderful at their job. About this time
I had perfected a system of my own for making controlled landings
using Gee only. This was partly to relieve the boredom and partly
as an ace in the hole in case the weather shut down while we were
airborne.

Although life at Swanton Morley was peaceful enough I was not
very happy there. The place was too full of ghosts and I had that
empty feeling inside which came from leaving squadron life. On a
squadron there is an almost unbearable tension but against this
there is the feeling that you are at the hub of things. This is what
the Royal Air Force is all about: every recruit training camp, every
technical training centre, the Empire Air Training Scheme, even
the Air Ministry itself, just exist to keep the squadrons flying. I
think that it was this feeling of being out of things, out of the war
even, that drove many aircrew to attempt a 'wangle' back to a
squadron even before they were ready for it.

May 1944 was notable for two things. The first was that, much to
my surprise, I was notified by the usual impersonal personal
telegram from the commander-in-chief I had been awarded the
DFC; the second was that, on 14 May, I was posted to A Flight of
the newly formed No. 2 Group Support Unit (GSU) – stationed at
Swanton Morley! This Group Support Unit was a new outfit that
had been formed to fill the gap between operational training units
and the squadrons now that the squadrons did not have the time

to carry out their own training programmes. Our role was to give the aircrews coming from OTU the operational training which they would normally receive on a squadron. Although we did not know it the day was drawing near when the squadrons of the 2nd Tactical Air Force would be over in France and unable to give their crews this necessary tuition. Our role was to deliver them to the squadrons ready for combat. The flight commander of A Flight was Squadron Leader Ritchie who had been my flight commander on No. 21 Squadron. I was given charge of the Navigation Section and, not having any equipment, I got it started up by borrowing a truck and going round the station pinching a table here and a chair there. It gave me a new interest in life and I was kept pretty busy getting a training programme knocked out.

My first two flights on 19 May were in an Oxford on Gee instruction, but on the 24th I flew with Squadron Leader Ritchie in a Mosquito Mk VI NS894, on a practice low-level formation. In this case it was a low level with a difference. We flew at the rear of the formation and I was continually disturbed by the danger horn blowing as Ritchie throttled back because the leader was flying too slowly. At 0 feet it is rather disconcerting to know that your pilot has just cut the throttles. Ritchie's language was colourful, but at least he knew how to fly. Half-way round the leading navigator got lost and we spent a fair amount of time at low level over various Midland towns. Eventually the formation arrived at Lasham, which was our destination, after having carried out a practice attack on an American airfield by mistake. I also flew with Squadron Leader Reeve in an Oxford on Gee instruction on the 31st; No. 1508 Flight had been disbanded and he was now an instructor with No. 2 GSU.

It was also in May that I attended an open air investiture to receive my DFC from the King. The investiture was held at Hartford Bridge which was the home of No. 138 Wing of the 2nd Tactical Air Force, the Boston and Mitchell boys. It was part of the fairy story that, because we were so busy operating against the enemy, the King was to come and make the awards 'in the field'.

The only snag was that all those concerned were, like myself, on rest, but no doubt it was good publicity for the long-suffering public. We were all issued with new battledress, which we had to return to stores afterwards, and our party set out from Swanton Morley in, of all things, a car! When we eventually reached Hartford Bridge we were paraded with a suitable backing of airmen and airwomen and there we stood for a very long time. When the King eventually arrived, complete with Service Police motor cyclists in a motorcade, I was pleased to hear him tear the top brass off a huge strip. Apparently his escort had arrived late. We had all been fitted up with a metal hook just below our medal ribbons on which His Majesty would hang our decorations. Most of those receiving awards were senior officers and there had been a lot of back slapping and hand shaking among them before the parade. There were only about ten of us lowly flying officers and, I particularly noticed, no NCOs, so we were feeling a bit out of all this happy reunion business. We filed up to receive our decorations in order of their importance and then in order of seniority so I was pretty well right at the back of the queue. I remember putting up a bit of a black by saying, over-loudly, to the flying officer behind me that it looked as though we would be unlucky and there would be only Air Force Crosses left by the time we got there. The fifteen or so wing commanders behind us waiting for Air Force Crosses gave me a very cold set of stares! Group Captain Peter Townsend was acting ADC to the King on this occasion.

The King stood on a carpet in front of which a white mark had been painted on the grass to which we all had to march. From time to time, in true Air Force fashion, officers halted short or over the mark and the King, who still seemed in a bad temper, would beckon his ADC and point this out to him. When at last my turn came I stood there and answered the stock question: 'How many operations have you done?' (If you had the DFM already you were warned that you would be asked 'How long have you been commissioned?') A wing commander I knew who had served a long time in the Middle East and had an accumulation of medals to collect told me that the King had felt this called for a little impromptu work, but his speech impediment prevented him from getting it out – so with great presence of mind the wing commander saluted smartly, right-turned and marched off. Unfortunately when my medal had been hooked on I was so intrigued by this, my one and only close contact with the King of Great Britain, that I just stood there very rudely having a jolly good stare until, with an impatient nod, I was dismissed back into the realms of the vast unknown. It was, I confess, very nice to go around wearing a medal, but I was always conscious of the fact that much better men had not got one, and the whole method of handing them out was viewed by most with great cynicism. On the way back to Swanton Morley Ritchie got roaring drunk and insisted on driving through London sitting on the bonnet of the car wearing his medal and waving a beer bottle at everybody, which was hardly the way a squadron leader in the Royal Air Force should behave.

Good news was swiftly followed by bad. After all my hard work getting the Navigation Section of No. 2 GSU into shape and the pride which I felt at being in charge of something for the first time in my Service career, along came a light lieutenant observer to take over the job. He had been a wing commander's navigator and had been handed the job by No. 2 Group. Not for the first time I was finding out that it is not what you know but who you know that counts in this world.

In June to emphasise our mobility the powers that be took us out of our comfortable quarters in the mess at Swanton Morley and moved us into tents on the far side of the airfield. Luckily for us it was a hot June, so life under canvas was quite pleasant. The following month I continued to fly in Oxford aircraft training observers in the use of Gee. It was dull, monotonous work but something happened to me that month which took my mind completely away from the day-to-day events – I met my future wife, who had just been invalided out of the ATS, heavy ack-ack division. The first night we walked home together she slipped her arm through mine and I am more than pleased to say that it has been there ever since.

August continued in exactly the same way as July. I was very happy for the first time in a long while, the only fly in the ointment being the efforts of Squadron Leader Ritchie to talk me into going back on operations with him. Apart from my normal duties I had also been made the unit's safety officer and had to give instruction in baling out and ditching drill. Needless to say I carried out these tasks with gusto and, looking back, I realise that I must have been a bit of a fanatic on these subjects. One thing that the crews did appreciate was a so-called survival camp which I managed to set up on a bank of the Norfolk Broads. Tents and rations were provided and we took the crews out for a stay of forty-eight hours, in which time they were supposed to use the dinghies I had given them. The sight of aircrew bods dressed in their yellow Mae Wests in one-man dinghies floating about on the Broads each with a pint mug in his hand and a load of beer bottles in the dinghy was a sight worth seeing. This camp was very popular and at least gave them a break from what was, after all, a very serious course. I had made contact with the Air-Sea Rescue Headquarters at Bircham Newton and used to take parties of aircrew over there by bus on rainy days when there was no flying. Here I actually met the pilot of the Hudson which had been bringing an airborne lifeboat out to the Americans we had been circling when we were shot down. He had first noticed a long white streak on the surface of the water, which had been us ditching, had then seen the German aircraft, so had turned for home and luckily got away unnoticed. I remember the feeling I had the first time I saw their write-up on my rescue in a file they kept of rescue operations; it concluded with the words: 'Only their grim determination to survive kept them alive.'

September followed the same pattern and I flew in Mitchells quite a few times with Flying Officer Parsons who had been a pilot on No. 226 Squadron while I was with them, but October brought a change. I was transferred from A Flight to C Flight of No. 2 GSU.

This meant that I was now in a section which concentrated wholly on radar training and I found myself flying once more in the good old Anson. My flight commander was a Squadron Leader Hart, known as 'Hawker' after that famous aircraft. He was a short, hook-nosed, red-faced, regular observer, very efficient at his job and a very kindly man.

On 12 October at 0945 hours I took off in Anson NK709 with Squadron Leader Reeve, my ex-CO of No. 1508 Flight, as pilot to fly to Benson, home of the RAF's photo-reconnaissance squadrons. At 1314 hours on the same day we took off from Benson to fly to Melsbroek (Brussels) with Group Captain Kippenberger as passenger. The group captain had such a quantity of luggage that I thought we would never get off the ground, and it was piled so high in our Anson that I had difficulty seeing over the top of it. It gave me the most peculiar feeling to be flying out across the North Sea at low level in broad daylight in an unarmed Anson, and I got quite an attack of the jitters when the Dutch coast loomed up ahead. Some of the Channel ports were still in the hands of the Germans and we had to give them a wide berth as they used to wait until an unwary aircraft was directly overhead at about 1,000 feet, which was the height at which we had to cross the coast, and then would let fly with everything they had. In this manner they accounted for a considerable number of Allied aircraft. The countryside was extensively flooded and looked most desolate. When we landed at Melsbroek I was very impressed with the German camouflage; even from ground level it was good. The flying control tower, for instance, had been built to represent a farmhouse complete with windows and doors, and made me realise that our bits of netting or splashes of zigzag paint were but a poor substitute.

The rest of the month, in which I clocked up 50 hours 25 minutes' flying time, was spent on Gee instruction with the exception of one trip to Vitry on 24 October in Anson MG565. This was the first time I had been able to study the French landscape at leisure, and the way the countryside was pock-marked with bomb craters was quite amazing.

The American daylight bomber offensive was in full swing and the Norfolk sky was filled with the vapour trails of the Americans as they climbed up from their bases and formed up into their massive armadas. When they returned we used to fly around from one great pillar of smoke to the next, which marked the grave of yet another Fortress or Liberator which had not made it. As they came in to land nearly every aircraft would be firing off red distress signals to denote that they had wounded on board. It was a truly impressive sight, and soon Norfolk was strewn with the wrecks of crashed American aircraft. A lot of the American casualties were caused by their habit of blazing away at German fighters diving through their formations irrespective of the hits they scored on their own aircraft which happened to get in the line of fire. The RAF method of strict fire control of the defence over the radio by the senior air gunner seemed unknown to them. The whole attitude of the Americans to both men and machines was radically different from ours, as the following incident shows.

One day watching the Liberators of Horsham St Faith taxiing round the perimeter track ready for an operational take off we were dismayed to see the nosewheel of the third aircraft from the front slowly collapse. Because the Liberator had a very short nosewheel the damage to the aircraft at this stage was only slight and consisted of an odd bent panel or so. If this had happened in the RAF it would most certainly have meant the cancellation of the operation in all but the gravest of situations while the senior engineering officer studied how best the aircraft could be raised without causing further damage. In this case, however, things happened with amazing speed. An American airman, who happened to be driving past in a tractor chewing gum and with one of those baseball-type caps stuck on the back of his head, stopped his tractor, reversed it up to the crippled bomber and, without a word to anyone, thrust a great hook into the nose, attached it to a cable on his tractor and with much banging, jerking and scraping, pulled the machine out of the line. Once it was clear the rest of the Liberators taxied past and took off leaving one aircraft behind, which was by now a complete write-off. The difference in attitudes stemmed, no doubt, from the very different quantities of both men and machines the two Allies were used to handling.

The expression 'round-the-clock bombing' could not be fully appreciated by anyone who had not lived in Norfolk or the surrounding area in those times. After the great American vapour trails had disappeared far out towards Germany and then back home and the glinting sun which had shone on their silver fuselages had sunk below the horizon a vast droning sound would be heard until the whole sky would resound with it as the hundreds of heavy bombers of Bomber Command set out on their individual lonely journeys. Sometimes, if they had a target deep in Germany and they set out just before sunset, you would see them dotted all over the sky as they set out into the sunset. Otherwise the sound could not be traced to any one quarter of the sky; the steady drone, drone, drone came from all quarters at once so that the very ground vibrated with the noise. Early in the morning this seemed to have a tired tone and from time to time you could detect a discordant note as damaged engines, out of tune with their fellows, made themselves heard like a beast in pain. The whole vast air offensive made me feel very humble and also made me feel that, now the tide had so obviously turned and the Allied cause was being sustained by such ever-increasing numbers of aircrew, they could very well do without my humble efforts in the combat zone.

I did a lot of flying over to the Continent, mainly Vitry, in November, ferrying replacement aircrew to their squadrons in Ansons. On the 4th we flew over twice in one day, doing 6 hours 10 minutes' flying. Despite the frequency of these flights I could not get used to the strange feeling of being able to fly in an unarmed aircraft over an area which had been so hotly contested such a short time before. On one trip to Melsbroek we ran into bad weather. My pilot was a Warrant Officer Whitwell who was an excellent pilot and we decided to try that most dangerous of operations, letting down through cloud. We sank lower and lower but the visibility ahead was still zero until, by peering vertically downwards, I suddenly saw hedges flashing past just below our propellers. We had to climb again hurriedly and divert to Vitry until the weather cleared. If there had been any high ground, or even a tall building, ahead, that would have been the end of us. We were lucky but I resolved never to attempt such a manoeuvre again as I could remember only too well friends of mine who had not been so lucky. Once, when returning across the Channel at 0 feet in poor visibility, we ran right into two destroyers which were lying heaved to. There was no time to turn away so we pulled up and flew right over their decks. Knowing how trigger-happy the Navy could be I sprang into action with the Verey pistol, which was mounted in the roof of the Anson, and set off three flares with the identification colours of the day. Looking back I saw that, as we were so low, the flares had come down on the deck of one of the destroyers, near the bows, and were burning merrily.

On 11 November I went on seven days' leave to get married.

Epilogue

In December 1944 No. 2 GSU moved to RAF Fersfield, near Diss, and at the beginning of the new year I returned to training navigators on Gee, in Ansons and Mitchells. I had now received my time promotion to flight lieutenant and had reached the dizzy heights I had envied so long ago as a trainee sergeant observer at Upwood. I had now been on rest for twelve months (flying a total of 394 hours 15 minutes) and had trained over one hundred navigators in the use of Gee.

On 21 March 1945 at 0945 hours I took off in Anson NK709 for a spot of Gee instruction, not realising that this was to be my last flight in the RAF as a crew member. The night before I had a very bad attack of asthma and my wife had to call out the station MO, complete with ambulance. He broke my attack, not without difficulty, and I was carted off to the station sick quarters. Things happened fairly swiftly after this – I was grounded, given a Medical Board, sent to the RAF Officers' Hospital at Blackpool and then invalided out. For me the war was over; the battle of the peace was just beginning.

Although I had been married for only a short time while serving in aircrew, it made me realise the great strain under which married aircrew must have lived compared with us 'happy bachelors', with only ourselves to worry about. True, we felt rather uncomfortable on leave when 'fussed over' by parents, but when have active young men ever worried much about their parents' feelings?

With the benefit of hindsight would I do the same thing again? Yes, without question, not because I was or am in any way brave or bloodthirsty but because if the day ever comes when the youth of this nation are not prepared to sacrifice their lives, if necessary, in the defence of the greatest country on earth we will no longer be that. Many believe that war is such an evil that under no circumstances should it ever happen again, but as long as evil persists in the world good men must stand up against it. The question is often asked 'Was the war worth it, what did we gain from it?' That is not the point, the point is that if a lot of fine men had not given their lives and we had lost the war, or not fought it, would the questioner like the life of a slave? It is also the fashion these days to denigrate the achievements of Bomber Command and to suggest that their activities were as bad as those of their enemies. This is to ignore the fact that they started it – we were just better at it than they were. I have never been able to understand how little seems to be known today about the hardships endured by the civilian population during those years. It is ironic in these days of much affluence the desire to protect our island, which was so fierce in those days, seems to have almost disappeared, swamped by the search for ever more affluence.

My lasting gratitude goes to the pre-war Regulars of the RAF. They were superbly trained and shockingly equipped and as a result died buying time for us to train and join them so that the fight could be won. My fear is that the Regulars of today may suffer the same fate, as we are the only country that never seems to learn the lessons of history. The only way we can have the things we want is to have the freedom to choose them, and we can never put too high a price on that freedom.

Looking back I realise that during training there was a challenge, a challenge not to fail, to pass the course and continue on with your fellow pupils, it was all very new, it was exciting! All the photographs you will ever see of a wartime course, be it Navy, Army or Air Force, show a group of young men, generally standing with arms folded, all with the same keen and happy look on their faces; on reading the text below there will often be the names of those who died, and that leads me to my final thoughts.

Why me? Why did I live when so many better and cleverer than me did not? Believe it or not that is what we, the survivors, often ask ourselves. Being a survivor makes you feel guilty, you ask yourself endless questions such as, 'Could I have done more to save the others?' or 'Was it my fault that it happened?' In aircrew a good crew had a bonding that in many ways was stronger than that of brothers; you trusted them with your life. To begin with you felt that you would all survive because you knew you were a good crew – it would always be the other fellow – then something happened and you suddenly knew that this was not so: if you were in the wrong piece of sky when the shell exploded it did not matter how good you were. Some aircrew went through several horrific experiences and despite this were eventually killed, others did one, two, or even three tours of operations without a scratch – why?

God alone knows.

Index